The New Rosary in Scripture

Biblical Insights for Praying the 20 Mysteries

Edward Sri

PUBLISHED BY ST. ANTHONY MESSENGER PRESS
CINCINNATI, OHIO

Scripture verses are from the *Revised Standard Version of the Bible,* copyright ©1946, 1952, 1957, 1965, 1966 by the Division of Christian Education of the National Council of Churches of Christ in the USA. Used by permission. Excerpts from the English translation of the *Catechism of the Catholic Church* for use in the United States of America Copyright 1994, United States Catholic Conference, Inc.—Libreria Editrice Vaticana. Used with Permission.

Cover design: Candle Light Studios

Library of Congress Cataloging-in-Publication Data

Sri, Edward P.
  The new Rosary in Scripture : biblical insights for praying the 20 mysteries / Edward Sri.
       p. cm.
Includes bibliographical references.
  ISBN 1-56955-384-X (alk. paper)
  1. Rosary. I. Title.
  BX2163.S65 2003
  242'.74—dc21

                                                            2003013161

ISBN-13: 978-1-56955-384-8
ISBN-10: 1-56955-384-X

Published by Servant Books, an imprint of St. Anthony Messenger Press,
28 W. Liberty St., Cincinnati, OH 45202
www.ServantBooks.org

Printed in the United States of America

09 10 11 12 9 8 7 6

To My Wife, Elizabeth

Contents

Acknowledgments

I would like to thank the many people who offered their prayers and encouragement for this project, especially my colleagues and students at Benedictine College. I am also particularly grateful to Bert Ghezzi at Servant Publications who first suggested that I write a book on the rosary in Scripture and to Curtis Mitch for his friendship and for his valuable feedback on this work.

Introduction

The New Mysteries: Why Now?

You know you are living in an historic moment when *USA Today* is teaching people how to pray the rosary.

Its October 17, 2002, edition featured an article that included a typical *USA Today* visual aid graphic but with very atypical content: a diagram of the rosary. The graphic offered clear instructions on how to pray the rosary, explaining which prayer—Our Father, Hail Mary, or Glory Be—should be recited with which bead. While one might expect to find such a picture and explanation in pamphlets in the back of a church, it was surprising to find it in the pages of the secular press, and no less, in one of our nation's most widely read newspapers.

What was the impulse for such catechetical instruction in this most unusual of settings?

Mysteries of Light

The day before the article's publication, Pope John Paul II began the twenty-fifth year of his papacy by dedicating the months from October 2002 to October 2003 as a "Year of the Rosary." In his apostolic letter *The Rosary of the Virgin Mary* (*Rosarium Virginis Mariae*), released that day, John Paul II called on Catholics in this period to renew their devotion to this traditional prayer. However, what grabbed the attention of *USA Today* and media throughout the world was the pope's extraordinary proposal to introduce a whole new set of mysteries for contemplation in the rosary: "the Mysteries of Light."

11

It is not every day that new mysteries are added to the rosary. In fact, the prayer's basic format had been in place since the sixteenth century. This structure included a series of prayers with reflections on the saving events surrounding the "Joyful Mysteries" of Christ's birth, the "Sorrowful Mysteries" of his passion and death, and the "Glorious Mysteries" of his resurrection.

In order to enter more fully into the life of Jesus through the rosary, the pope suggested that Catholics also reflect on the mysteries of Christ's public ministry. He thus proposed the following five scenes to be contemplated: (1) Christ's baptism; (2) the wedding feast at Cana; (3) the proclamation of the kingdom; (4) the Transfiguration; and (5) the institution of the Eucharist. By focusing our attention on his public ministry, these new Mysteries of Light make a stronger connection between Christ's childhood in the Joyful Mysteries and the culmination of his messianic mission in the Sorrowful Mysteries.

In the months following the release of this letter on the rosary, one question many Catholics asked was simply *why?* Why did John Paul II dedicate the twenty-fifth year of his pontificate as a Year of the Rosary? Why was he so concerned that Catholics deepen their commitment to this devotion? And most of all, why did he add these new Mysteries of Light?

The pope gave at least three reasons for the timeliness of his proposal. These correspond to three crises he was seeing today: (1) a crisis of the rosary within the Catholic Church, (2) a crisis of peace in the world, and (3) a crisis of the family in the home.

A Crisis of the Rosary

In his apostolic letter John Paul II speaks of "a certain crisis of the rosary." He points out that this important devotion from our tradition has been misunderstood, pushed to the side, or even forgotten in our present era. He says the rosary today "can risk being wrongly devalued, and therefore no longer taught to the younger generation."[1]

A number of years ago I stopped at a church in Michigan during my lunch hour to pray the rosary. As I was praying, an older woman walked in and saw me kneeling with my rosary beads in hand. She looked confused, concerned, and very curious about what I was doing. After a few Hail Marys I began to feel uncomfortable when I noticed she was still staring at me. She finally walked up to me and asked, "Are you praying the *rosary?*" I told her that I was, and in response, she said to me, "Wow, you must be uneducated!"

I was not sure what she intended by that statement, but I felt somewhat insulted. I asked her, "What do you mean by that?"

She then hesitatingly began to tell me her story: "Well, I have always prayed the rosary. And I was here in this same church yesterday praying the rosary just like you are, and a priest walked in and asked me why I was doing that. He told me that the rosary is only for the uneducated people and that educated Catholics don't need it anymore."

She then looked down at the ground and sincerely, but somewhat embarrassedly, said, "I guess ... I guess since I don't have as much education as other people ... I guess that's why I still pray the rosary." Then, looking back at me, she said, "But you ... you look like you'd be educated, so I was surprised to see *you* praying it!"

I sympathized with this good, pious woman who had been humiliated for praying the rosary. But perhaps even more, I felt for the poor, misguided priest who had made these unfortunate comments. I share this story because it exemplifies, at least to some degree, the way the rosary is misunderstood and devalued by many Catholics today—by laity and even some priests and religious. And this lack of appreciation for the rosary has had its effects. According to a 2001 poll by the Center for Applied Research for the Apostolate at Georgetown University, the majority of Catholics in the United States do not pray the rosary on a regular basis. Only 27 percent said they pray the rosary several times a month. That is in contrast to 33 percent who said they pray it only a few times a year, and 39 percent who said they never pray it at all.[2]

Admittedly, most Catholics in the United States do not have much excitement about the rosary, understanding about its meaning, or even familiarity with how to pray it. In the subsequent chapters of this book we will explore many of the good questions people have about the rosary and shed light on some common misconceptions about this devotion. At this point, however, I simply wish to highlight that John Paul II seemed right to be concerned that this important part of our tradition is not being passed on effectively to the next generation. While it is true that some younger Catholics have grown up with the rosary in their homes or in their Catholic schools and parishes, this does not seem to be the case for many others.

For example, some of my college students have told me that they grew up thinking the rosary was something Catholics only prayed in front of dead people. For them it was the funeral home prayer. Other students had the impression that the rosary was just a prayer for the elderly men and women who come early to church on Sunday. Still others have said they went through twelve years of Catholic schools without ever learning how to pray the rosary. I would bet many other Catholic university students across the country would offer similar testimonies about a lack of familiarity or understanding of the rosary.

It thus seems fitting that John Paul II would describe the current situation as a "crisis of the rosary." His apostolic letter is, in part, a response to this crisis. In it, he invites Catholics to rediscover the treasures of this devotion. And he says the addition of the new Mysteries of Light is meant to give the rosary "fresh life" and "enkindle renewed interest in the rosary's place within Christian spirituality."[3]

A Crisis in the World

The grave threats to world peace at the start of the third millennium represent a second reason John Paul II called for a renewal of rosary devotion. In this letter on the rosary he mentions the terrifying attacks of September 11, 2001, as well as other scenes of violence and bloodshed throughout the world. One gets the sense that John Paul II was greatly concerned that the world might be on the brink of a great disaster. With unusual candor he says, "The grave challenges confronting the world at the start of this new Millennium lead us to think that *only an intervention from on high,* capable of guiding the hearts of those living in situations of conflict and those governing the destinies of nations, can give reason to hope for a brighter future."[4]

Did you catch that? Like a prophet, John Paul II seemed to think that only God's intervention can keep the turmoil of the world from exploding into a terrifying conflict. And he calls Catholics to turn to that divine power by praying for peace and in particular, by praying *the rosary* for peace.

According to the pope, the rosary is a most fitting prayer for peace, because it leads us to contemplate Christ, the Prince of Peace. "How could one possibly contemplate the mystery of the Child of

Bethlehem, in the Joyful Mysteries, without experiencing the desire to welcome, defend, and promote life and to shoulder the burdens of suffering children all over the world? How could one follow in the footsteps of Christ the Revealer in the Mysteries of Light without resolving to bear witness to his Beatitudes in daily life? And how could one contemplate Christ carrying the cross and Christ crucified without feeling the need to act as a Simon of Cyrene for our brothers and sisters weighed down by grief or despair? Finally, how could one possibly gaze upon the glory of the risen Christ or of Mary Queen of Heaven without yearning to make this world more beautiful, more just, more closely conformed to God's plan?"[5]

In reflecting on the mysteries of Jesus Christ with his blessed mother in the rosary, we ask Mary—the one who brought the Prince of Peace into this world two thousand years ago in Bethlehem—to pray for us, that peace may be born anew in our world today.

A Crisis in the Family

A third reason the pope dedicated the Year of the Rosary was for a renewal of family life. The family, the most basic and most important institution of society, is under attack as never before, and this has had tragic consequences. Broken marriages and broken families have led to broken hearts and broken lives. While the culture offers less and less support for traditional marriage and family life, ideological movements push to redefine what a marriage even is. The pope feared for the future of this "fundamental and indispensable institution and, with it, for the future of society as a whole."[6]

In his document on the rosary John Paul II mentions that one of the greatest challenges to fostering strong bonds of love in the home today is that family members rarely have meaningful conversation with each other.[7] In our society we often are so busy doing other things that many families do not take time to really talk to each other, look each other in the eye, get into each other's lives, and know each other's hearts. Even in good Christian homes parents stay late at work, and children frequently are away for athletic events or other activities. Meanwhile, the few family members remaining at home often are busy "doing their own thing," whether it be surfing the Internet, working on a project, talking on the phone, or playing computer games. In many cases, what isolates family members from each other the most is the television. As John Paul II observes, "Families seldom manage to come together, and the rare occasions when they do are often taken up with watching television."[8]

As a tool to help families gather around something more edifying and life-giving than the TV screen, the pope recommends a return to the traditional Catholic practice of the family rosary. He asks families to consider praying the rosary together in the home: "To return to the recitation of the family Rosary means filling daily life with very different images, images of the mystery of salvation: the image of the Redeemer, the image of his most Blessed Mother."[9] Indeed, what images would be better to present to the eyes of our souls and the souls of our children: the images of Jay Leno, Oprah Winfrey, and the nightly news from television or the images of Jesus, Mary, and Joseph in the mysteries of salvation?

The pope quotes the adage "The family that prays together stays together" and adds that the rosary can help strengthen the bonds of love in the home in a unique way. By constantly presenting images from the life of Jesus—his compassion, humility, generosity, patience, forgiveness, and selflessness—the rosary challenges us to imitate his love in our own homes. "Individual family members, in turning their eyes toward Jesus, also regain the ability to look one another in the eye, to communicate, to show solidarity, to forgive one another and to see their covenant of love renewed in the Spirit of God."[10]

While the pope admits that bringing children together for this regular "pause for prayer" is not the solution to every problem in the family, he does remind us that the rosary is a profound "spiritual aid which should not be underestimated."[11]

From John Paul II's Heart

Finally, another timely reason John Paul II inaugurated the Year of the Rosary on October 16, 2002, is that this date marked the beginning of his twenty-fifth year as the pope. Shortly after he assumed the office of Peter in 1978, he said the rosary was his favorite prayer and entrusted his entire papacy to the "daily rhythm of the rosary." Then, in this 2002 letter on the rosary, he looked back over his pontificate and said this prayer had been a tremendous source of strength and guidance for him in the many challenges he faced while serving as the pope. In reading this letter, one gets the sense that he entered the twenty-fifth year of his papacy wanting to leave the Church at least one last great gift, something personal and springing from his own heart: the rosary.

Twenty-five years later, thinking back over the difficulties which have also been part of my exercise of the [papacy], I feel the need to say once more, as a warm invitation to everyone to experience it personally: the Rosary does indeed "mark the rhythm of human life," bringing it into harmony with the "rhythm" of God's own life, in the joyful communion of the Holy Trinity, our life's destiny and deepest longing.[12]

Here we encounter one of the most remarkable aspects of this apostolic letter: its highly personal tone. Most high-level papal documents remain primarily on the theological and pastoral plane. However, in writing about the rosary in this document, John Paul II bares a part of his soul to the world as he shares about his own devotion to this Marian prayer. For example, consider his following comments:

> From my youthful years this prayer has held an important place in my spiritual life.... The Rosary has accompanied me in moments of joy and in moments of difficulty. To it I have entrusted any number of concerns: in it I have always found comfort.[13]

To feel the full weight of this statement, we must put these words about *finding comfort in moments of difficulty* within the context of John Paul II's life. Here is a man who lost his mother when he was in third grade and his father when he was twenty. He almost lost his own life during the Nazi occupation of Poland, first, when he was struck down by a German truck, and on another occasion, when the Gestapo searched his house but did not find him hiding in a basement closet. After working in the underground cultural resistance to the Nazi regime as a layman, he later as a priest and bishop openly confronted the many evils of a communist government which was trying to turn Poland into an atheistic society. One must think of these and many other trials from his life as part of the background to his words, "The Rosary has accompanied me in moments of joy and in *moments of difficulty*. To it I have entrusted any number of concerns: *in it I have always found comfort*."

These are not the words of an abstract theologian or an out-of-touch pastor who is exhorting us to cling to our beads merely for the sake of saving a pious tradition that he fears is in danger of going out of style. No, these words flow from the heart of a man who experienced much suffering in his own life and found the rosary to be a source of strength and hope in times of trial. Like a good father, he wanted to share with us the spiritual strength and comfort that he found in this prayer.

This may be the most important context for understanding the pope's urgent plea for Catholics to rediscover the rosary. In times of trouble, John Paul II always turned to the rosary, bringing the drama of his own life into harmony with the life of God. Today, while the world's peace may be gravely threatened and family life may be suffering tremendously, the pope's words encourage us to do what he himself always did in times of crisis: turn to Jesus in the rosary. He exhorts all of us—whether priests or laity, young or old, families or single people—to take up the rosary again and unite our lives more with Christ's by reflecting on the mysteries of salvation in this prayer.

In the following pages we will explore the pope's very timely—but what also are sure to be known as timeless—insights on the meaning of the rosary and how we can pray it with greater devotion. In the first chapter we will address common apologetic and historical questions people have about Mary and the rosary, such as "Why do Catholics give so much attention to Mary?" "Why do they pray to her?" "What is the purpose of all the repetitious prayer in the rosary?" and "What are the origins of the rosary?"

In the second chapter we will discuss some common difficulties people face when praying the rosary and consider ten practical suggestions from John Paul II on how to pray the rosary in a way that leads our hearts closer to Christ.

The following four chapters offer scriptural reflections on each of the Joyful, Luminous, Sorrowful, and Glorious Mysteries in turn. These reflections are intended to enrich the reader's contemplation of

Christ by unearthing some of the historical context, Old Testament background, and spiritual meaning of the biblical texts related to the mysteries of the rosary.

And finally, chapter seven provides a scriptural rosary. This serves as a compendium of Biblical verses readers can use as a resource to incorporate more Scripture into their praying of the rosary.

Let us now take up John Paul II's call to rediscover the rosary in light of Scripture, in harmony with the liturgy, and in the context of our daily lives.

ONE

Common Questions About
Mary and the Rosary

W hy do Catholics give so much attention to Mary?"

This is a question I have heard many times—from my Protestant friends and even a few Catholics. For some people, Catholic devotion to Mary can be scandalous. They would say, If Christians are called to worship Jesus Christ, why do so many Catholic practices seem to distract us from a personal relationship with Jesus by focusing so much on Mary? While Mary may be a fine woman, a holy role model, and blessed to have served as the mother of the messiah, she is *not* God. So why do Catholics treat her as if she were on par with God himself?

I can appreciate these concerns. After all, Catholicism does highlight Mary's role in God's plan of salvation more than any other religion in the world. What other faith has so many statues, paintings, icons, and stained glass windows depicting Mary? What other religion proclaims as many doctrines that specifically involve the mother of Jesus (such as the Immaculate Conception, her perpetual virginity, and her assumption into heaven)? What other faith has so many songs dedicated to Mary (such as "Immaculate Mary" and "Hail Holy Queen") and so many prayers addressed to her (such as the Hail Mary, the Memorare, and the Angelus)?

Then, of course, there is the rosary. This devotion stands out as one of the most perplexing of all Catholic practices involving Mary. In this prayer Catholics recite five sets of ten Hail Marys. Each set, called a "decade," is introduced by the Our Father and concluded with praise of the Holy Trinity in a prayer known as the Glory Be. From an outsider's perspective, at the end of each decade of the rosary the score seems to be:

God the Father: 1
The Holy Trinity: 1
Mary: 10

Some may wonder why so much weight is placed on Mary—and not on God—in the rosary. At best, all this repetitive attention given to Mary seems to be unbalanced and distracting us from a relationship with Christ. At worst, this prayer seems to be a form of idolatry, treating Mary as if she were more important than God himself.

Before discussing the rosary itself, I want to address the uneasiness some people feel about this traditional Catholic prayer. In this chapter we will consider seven common questions about Mary and the rosary. It is my hope that addressing these questions will help us better appreciate the beauty of Marian devotion in our own lives and explain it more effectively to others.

1. "Why Do Catholics Worship Mary?"

In short, Catholics do *not* worship Mary.

To answer this question more fully, we must distinguish between "honor" and "worship." To honor someone is to show the person respect, recognizing a particular quality or excellence they have achieved in their lives. Worship denotes the homage and praise we give to God alone for who he is as the divine being.

Christians honor people all the time. We honor students for good grades by placing them on the dean's list. We honor employees by giving them a pay raise. We honor athletes by presenting them with trophies, gold medals, and Super Bowl rings. *When we as Christians honor someone, ultimately, we recognize the great things God has accomplished in their lives.*

For example, as a professor, I *honor* my students when they graduate from college. I may applaud them at their commencement and congratulate them for completing their degrees. But I do not fall down on my knees and *worship* them as they walk out of the graduation ceremony! At the same time, such honor does not in any manner take away from the worship I should give to God. In fact, it enhances that worship because in honoring my students I am praising the one true God for giving them the talents and graces they needed to complete their college education.

Similarly, Catholics *honor* Mary and the saints, but they do not *worship* them. And honoring Mary in no way distracts from our worship of God, but actually enables us to praise God all the more. If someone wants to praise an artist, he does so by admiring his art. Leonardo da Vinci would not be upset with people who admire the gaze of his Mona Lisa, and Michelangelo would not be angry with people who admire his Last Judgment scene in the Sistine Chapel. No artist would rush into a museum and say, "Stop looking at my works of art! Stop talking about my paintings! You should be giving all your attention to *me!*" Rather, the artist is praised when his masterpieces are recognized and celebrated.

In a similar way, God is a divine artist, and his spiritual masterpieces are the saints. The saints are men and women who have been completely transformed by God's saving grace. We give God great praise when we thank him for the work of salvation he has accomplished in their lives.

Furthermore, taking time to recognize God's works in this world is very biblical. The scriptural writers, in fact, were very comfortable with admiring the beauty of God's creation. Psalm 104, for example, praises

God for the sun, the moon, the mountains, and the seas. Such recognition does not get in the way of our worshiping God but rather allows us to praise him even more by thanking him for the splendor of his creation.

If the Bible encourages us to praise God for his *natural* works of creation, how much more should we praise him for his *supernatural* works—for taking weak, fragile human beings and transforming them by his grace into holy sons and daughters of God.

When Catholics honor the saints, therefore, it is as if we are saying, "Praise be to you, Jesus, for what you did in the life of St. Paul!" or, "Thank you, Lord, for giving us St. Francis of Assisi as a model of holiness." Not only is it OK to honor Mary and the rest of the saints in this way, but we actually give God more praise when we recognize his redemptive work perfected in them.

2. "Why Do Catholics Pray to Mary?"

It may be better to say that Catholics do not pray *to* Mary, but we ask her to pray for us.

Yet some people may wonder, "Why not go to God directly?" After all, St. Paul taught that "there is one mediator between God and men, the man Jesus Christ" (1 Tm 2:5). Why do Catholics place Mary as an extra layer of mediation between men and God?

First, Christ's role as the "one mediator between God and men" in no way excludes the notion of Christians praying for one another.[1] In fact, Paul himself instructs Christians to intercede for one another (see 1 Tm 2:1). He even commands that people pray for him and his ministry: "You also must help us by prayer, so that many will give thanks on our behalf for the blessing granted us in answer to many prayers" (2 Cor 1:11). Paul's asking other Christians to pray for him seems quite natural. No one would accuse him of "not going directly to God" with his needs.

Clearly, the importance of Christians praying for each other is rooted in Scripture. And once we understand the profound communion existing between the saints in heaven and Christians here on earth, then the notion of Mary and the saints interceding for us will make a lot of sense.

The saints are our brothers and sisters in Christ who have gone before us. They have faced many of the struggles and trials we endure as Christians, and they have made it to the other side. Though they have died and gone to heaven, they have not been disconnected from God's family; they continue to be united to us through our common bond in Christ.

Furthermore, from a biblical perspective, though they have left this world, the saints are not "dead" but spiritually alive in the arms of God (Lk 20:38) and, in a sense, closer to us now than when they were on the earth. Indeed, the Letter to the Hebrews portrays the assembly of the saints in heaven not as a congregation far removed from the events of this world, but as a "great cloud of witnesses" that surrounds us in the drama of our daily lives (see Heb 12:1). As our older brothers and sisters in Christ, they continue to pray for us that we may persevere in the faith and one day join them in heaven (see Rv 5:8; 8:3).

Whether it be among Christians here on earth or with the saints in heaven, intercession is a way that we show our love for God and build up the body of Christ. When someone asked Jesus what were the greatest of the commandments, he responded: "You shall love the Lord your God with all your heart ... [and] love your neighbor as yourself" (Mt 22:37, 39). The Christian life can be summed up in these two themes, love of God and love of neighbor. In fact, we show our love for God by loving our neighbor. And one of the best ways we can grow in fellowship with our neighbor is through prayer: praying for others and sharing our needs with them so they might pray for us.

This is why seeking the intercession of Mary and the saints in no way distracts us from our relationship with God, but deepens our unity in God's family. God does not get jealous when we ask others to pray for us. For example, as a father, I am delighted when I see my children getting along so well that they turn to each other with their needs. Imagine if my son Paul were to ask his older sister Madeleine to help him count or help him say his prayers and I were to get angry with him, saying, "Paul, I feel so left out! Why are you asking your sister for help? Why don't you come to me directly with your needs?" Such an attitude would be strange indeed! As a father, I do not view their love for each other as competition for love and attention that should be given to me. Rather, I rejoice all the more when I see my children asking each other for help and lovingly responding to each other's needs.

In a similar way, our heavenly Father rejoices when he sees his sons and daughters loving each other so much that they ask each other for prayer and intercede for each other's needs. That is why the real question is not, "Is it OK to ask Mary and the saints to pray for us?" but rather, "Do you want to love God with all your heart?" We love God by loving all our brothers and sisters, including Mary and the saints, and we deepen our Christian fellowship by praying for one another and asking each other for prayer (see *CCC*, 957).[2]

3. Why the Hail Mary? Why Not a Christ-Centered Prayer?

At first glance the Hail Mary seems to be primarily about Mary. However, John Paul II emphasizes that this prayer is meant to focus our attention on Jesus Christ. "Although the repeated *Hail Mary* is addressed directly to Mary, it is to Jesus that the act of love is ultimately directed."[3]

We can see this in the first part of this prayer, which is drawn from the words that the angel Gabriel and Elizabeth used to greet the mother of the Messiah. These words do not focus primarily on Mary but on what John Paul II calls "the wonder of heaven and earth" over the mystery of the Incarnation taking place inside her. Gabriel—representing heaven—is in awe over the fact that God is about to enter Mary's womb and thus says to her: "Hail, full of grace, the Lord is with you" (Lk 1:28). Similarly, Elizabeth—representing earth—recognizes the mystery of Christ in Mary and says, "Blessed are you among women, and blessed is the fruit of your womb" (Lk 1:42).

By repeating these Biblical words in the Hail Mary, we participate in heaven and earth's joyful response to the mystery of God becoming man. As the pope explains, "These words ... could be said to give a glimpse of God's own wonderment as he contemplates his 'master-piece'—the Incarnation of the Son in the womb of the Virgin Mary.... The repetition of the *Hail Mary* in the Rosary gives us a share in God's own wonder and pleasure: in jubilant amazement we acknowledge the greatest miracle of history."[4]

After these opening lines, we come to the climax of the Hail Mary: "And blessed is the fruit of thy womb, *Jesus.*" John Paul II says that Jesus' holy name not only serves as the hinge joining the two parts of the Hail Mary but also is this prayer's very "center of gravity."[5] Indeed, the Hail Mary is meant to lead us to the person of Jesus, and at the center of this prayer we speak his sacred name.

We should never neglect the power of Christ's name—the only name under heaven by which we may hope in salvation (see Acts 4:12). From a biblical perspective, the very fact that we can even call upon the name of Jesus is astonishing. In the Old Testament the Jews approached God's name ("Yahweh") with so much reverence that eventually their tradition even avoided saying it. Instead they often called on God in prayer using the less personal title "Lord." However, since God has entered into humanity in Christ, we now have the privilege of calling on the personal name of the Lord, "Jesus" (*CCC*, 2666). Christians throughout the centuries have found in the name of Jesus a source of strength and meditation. The Hail Mary leads us to that divine source as we utter the sacred name at the center of this prayer.

In the last part of the Hail Mary we entrust our lives to Mary's intercession: "Holy Mary, mother of God, pray for us sinners, now and at the hour of our death. Amen." Even this part of the Hail Mary is meant to lead us to Christ. Here we ask Mary to pray for us to be faithful in our walk with the Lord, now and up to the moment of our death. As a model disciple of Christ, Mary consented to God's will when the angel Gabriel appeared to her (see Lk 1:38), and she persevered in faith throughout her life (see Jn 19:25-27; Acts 1:14). Consequently, she is the ideal person to be praying for us, praying that we may walk in faith as she did. The *Catechism of the Catholic Church* explains, "She prays for us as she prayed for herself: 'Let it be to me according to your word.' By entrusting ourselves to her prayer, we abandon ourselves to the will of God together with her: 'Thy will be done'" (*CCC*, 2677).

4. "Isn't the Rosary 'Vain Repetition'?"

In the Sermon on the Mount Jesus said, "And in praying do not heap up empty phrases as the Gentiles do; for they think that they will be heard for their many words. Do not be like them, for your Father knows what you need before you ask him" (Mt 6:7-8).

For some people the rosary appears to be the kind of repetitious prayer Jesus was condemning. With Hail Mary after Hail Mary, it may seem to be a dry, mechanical way of praying to God. It is thus often alleged that the rosary is "vain repetition," not true, intimate prayer flowing from the heart. Shouldn't Christians speak more openly to

Jesus rather than relying on formulas repeated over and over again?

In response, first, we must point out that Jesus does not condemn *all* types of repetition in prayer. Rather, he is criticizing the gentile practice of reciting endless formulas and divine names in order to say the right words that would force the gods to answer their petitions. Jesus condemns this pagan approach of trying to get God to answer their prayers through magical formulas. He challenges us to approach our Heavenly Father, not like the pagans do their deities, but rather in confident trust that "your Father knows what you need before you ask him" (Mt 6:8). Indeed, he knows what we need better than we do and is providing for those needs even before we realize them ourselves (see Mt 6:25-34).

Moreover, we know Jesus cannot be condemning all forms of repetition because, in the very next verse, he gives us a formula prayer to recite: the Our Father. Jesus says, "Pray then like this: Our Father, who art in heaven, hallowed be thy name...." (Mt 6:9-13). Furthermore, Jesus himself repeats his prayers. In the Garden of Gethsemane, Jesus spoke the same prayer three times: "leaving them again, he went away and prayed for the third time, saying the same words" (Mt 26:44). No one would accuse Jesus of vain repetition!

Similarly, in the Old Testament, parts of Psalm 118 are structured around the repeated phrase "his steadfast love endures forever," and the Book of Daniel presents the three men in the fiery furnace constantly repeating the phrase, "sing praise to him and highly exalt him forever" (see Dn 3:52-68). God does not condemn these ancient Jews for "vain repetition" but rather looks favorably on their prayers and answers them in their time of need (see Ps 118:21).

In the New Testament, the Book of Revelation describes how the four living creatures repeat the same prayer of praise for all eternity. Gathered around God's throne, "day and night they never cease to sing, 'Holy, holy, holy, is the Lord God Almighty, who was and is and is to come!'"(Rv 4:8). Thus the very worship of God in heaven involves words of holy praise that are repeated without end. In sum, although the pagan approach of trying to manipulate God by *vain* repetition is always wrong, proper repetitious prayer is very biblical and pleasing to God.

5. But What Is the Purpose of Repetitious Prayers?

We may still wonder *why* there is so much repetition in the rosary.

The purpose of repeating prayers is not repetition for its own sake. Rather, the peaceful rhythm created by reciting familiar words from Scripture is meant to slow down our minds and spirits so that we can prayerfully reflect on different aspects of Christ's life.

The pope notes in his letter that this devotion is similar to the "Jesus Prayer" that people have recited for centuries. In this prayer, Christians slowly repeat the words "Jesus Christ, Son of God, have mercy on us," often following the rhythm of their breathing. The lingering pace of this prayer whispered over and over again is meant to calm the mind so that we may be more disposed to meet God himself in prayer. It helps us follow the exhortation of Psalm 46:10: "Be still, and know that I am God."

The succession of Hail Marys in the rosary is meant to achieve the same purpose. One Catholic theologian explains it like this: "Masters in the Buddhist tradition of meditation speak of 'calming the monkey mind.' This means the settling of the superficial mind which dances and darts from preoccupation to preoccupation and whose concerns tend to dominate our consciousness: 'What is my next appointment? Where do I go next? What did she mean by that?' In order to open up the deepest ground of the soul ... the mind must be, at least for a time, quelled. In the rosary meditation, the mantra of the repeated Hail

Marys quiets the monkey mind, compelling it to cede place to deeper reaches of the psyche."[6]

On another level, the pope encourages us to view the repetition of Hail Marys not as a superficial, mechanical exercise, which indeed would be rather boring and empty of life. Instead, the repetition of prayers should be understood within the context of a relationship of love. For example, I may tell my wife several times a day, "I love you." Sometimes I say these words to her as I am going out the door for work in the morning. Other times I whisper them just before we fall asleep at night. On special occasions I may write these words in a card. When we are out for dinner on a "date," I may look her in the eyes and say, "I love you." Although she has heard me repeat these same words to her thousands of times, never once has she complained, "Stop saying the same thing over and over again!... I can't take all this vain repetition!"

In an intimate, personal relationship such as marriage, two people may repeat to each other certain expressions of love, but each time the same words express the heartfelt affection the people have for one another. Indeed, repetition is part of the language of love.

This is the proper context for understanding the repeated prayers in the rosary. We have an intimate, personal relationship with Jesus Christ. In reciting the Hail Mary throughout the rosary we participate over and over again in the wonder-filled response of Gabriel and Elizabeth to the mystery of Christ. Bead after bead, we ask Mary to pray for us that we may be drawn closer to her son. And most of all, prayer after prayer, *we affectionately repeat the name of our Beloved* in the very center of each Hail Mary: "Blessed is the fruit of thy womb, *Jesus ... Jesus ... Jesus.*" Indeed, the name of Jesus, spoken with tender love, becomes the heartbeat of the entire rosary. This is why John Paul II says the rosary should be thought of as "an outpouring of that love which tirelessly returns to the person loved with expressions similar in their content but ever fresh in terms of the feeling pervading them.... To understand the Rosary, one has to enter into the psychological dynamic proper to love."[7]

6. What Is the Purpose of "the Mysteries"?

Pope Paul VI once said, "Without contemplation, the Rosary is a body without a soul, and its recitation runs the risk of becoming a mechanical repetition of formulas."[8] The "body" of the rosary is the prayers we recite with our lips (Our Father, Hail Mary, Glory Be), while its "soul" is our contemplation of the mysteries of Christ. Up to this point we have discussed primarily the body of the rosary. Now let us consider its soul.

With each decade of the rosary (each set of ten Hail Marys), we are to reflect on a different aspect of Christ's life and work of salvation. We move from the Joyful Mysteries, in which we reflect on the events surrounding the birth of Jesus; to the Mysteries of Light, where we meditate on Christ's public ministry; to the Sorrowful Mysteries of his passion and death; and finally to the Glorious Mysteries, where we reflect on Jesus' resurrection triumph. When praying the rosary, it is as if we were looking at "pictures" from the life and mission of Jesus Christ, from his childhood and ministry as an adult to his death and resurrection at the culmination of his messianic mission.[9]

This is why John Paul II said the rosary is truly a Christ-centered prayer. It is "a compendium" of the entire gospel because it presents us with images from God's plan of redemption as fulfilled in Jesus.[10] By continuously reflecting on the mysteries, we can participate today in those saving events made present to us. Thus the rhythm of the rosary can begin to shape the daily rhythm of our lives. John Paul II says, "[B]y immersing us in the mysteries of the Redeemer's life, it ensures that what he has done. . . is profoundly assimilated and shapes our existence."[11]

The repetition of the Hail Mary is meant to serve this purpose. Since the Hail Mary is a Biblical prayer centered on Christ, it is fitting that the mysteries of salvation pass before the eyes of the soul against the backdrop of this prayer. As Pope Paul VI once said, "As a Gospel prayer, centered on the mystery of the redemptive Incarnation, the Rosary is therefore a prayer with a clearly Christological orientation. Its most characteristic element, in fact, the litany-like succession of *Hail Marys,* becomes in itself an unceasing praise of Christ, who is the ultimate object both of the angel's announcement and the greeting of the mother of John the Baptist: 'Blessed is the fruit of your womb' (Lk 1:42)."[12]

7. How Did the Rosary Come to Be?

According to one tradition, the rosary's defining moment came during an apparition of Mary to St. Dominic around the year 1221. While Dominic was combating a popular heresy in France called Albigensianism, Mary appeared to him and gave him the rosary. She told him to teach people this devotion and promised that his apostolic efforts would be blessed with much success if he did. Whatever one makes of this tradition, Dominic's followers in the religious order he founded (the Dominicans) clearly played a major role in promoting the rosary throughout the world in the early years of this devotion.

"Poor Man's Breviary." What is certain about the development of the rosary is its roots in the liturgical prayer of the Church. In the medieval period there was a desire to give the laity a form of common prayer similar to that found in the monasteries. Monastic prayer was structured around the Psalter—the recitation of all 150 psalms from the Bible. At that time, however, most laity could not afford a Psalter, and most could not even read. As a parallel to the monastic reading of the 150 psalms, the practice developed of laity praying the Our Father 150 times throughout the day. This devotion came to be known as "the Poor Man's Breviary," and the laity eventually were given beads to help them count their prayers.

Repeating the Hail Mary. Marian devotion followed a similar pattern. Gabriel's words "Hail Mary, full of grace, the Lord is with thee" from Luke 1:28 sometimes were read in the monasteries at the end of a psalm, showing how the psalms found fulfillment in the New Testament with the coming of Christ through the Virgin Mary. Some laity began to recite these words in the manner of the Our Father— 150 times while counting their prayers on beads. In repeating the words of Gabriel, they were reliving the joy of the Annunciation and celebrating the mystery of God becoming man in Mary's womb.

Christians linked this prayer with Elizabeth's words to Mary at the Visitation: "Blessed art thou among women, and blessed is the fruit of thy womb" (Lk 1:42). Finally, with the addition of the name *Jesus* to this prayer in the thirteenth century, the first half of the Hail Mary was in place. This early form of the Hail Mary was recited 150 times on the beads. By the fifteenth century the 150 Hail Marys had been divided into sets of ten known as "decades," with an Our Father at the beginning of each.

Meditating on Mysteries. There was another line of development in monastic prayer that eventually led to the practice of contemplating Christ's life while reciting Hail Marys in the rosary. Some monasteries began associating the psalms with an aspect of Jesus' life. At the end of each psalm, they would recite a phrase relating that psalm to the life of Jesus or Mary. Taken together, these phrases formed a brief life of Christ and his mother.

A devotion that joined fifty of these phrases with the praying of fifty

Hail Marys began in the early fifteenth century. However, since fifty points of reflection generally could not be recalled without a book, the devotion was simplified by reducing the meditation points to fifteen, with one for every decade. Thus, by the end of the fifteenth century, the basic structure of the rosary was in place: Our Fathers dividing decades of Hail Marys with meditations on the life of Christ and Mary.

In the sixteenth century the sets of five Joyful, five Sorrowful, and five Glorious Mysteries as we know them today began to emerge. Also, the vocal prayers of the rosary were finalized. The Glory Be was added to the end of every decade, and the second half of the Hail Mary was formalized: "Holy Mary, mother of God, pray for us sinners now and at the hour of our death. Amen." In 1569, Pope St. Pius V officially approved the rosary in this form of decades of Hail Marys introduced by the Our Father and concluded with the Glory Be.

The New Mysteries. While there have been various developments in the way people have prayed the rosary in different parts of the world over the last four centuries, none have been as momentous as John Paul II's proposal to the universal Church to add the new Mysteries of Light. It should be emphasized, however, that these new mysteries were presented as a proposal. The pope was careful to stress that their addition should not supersede any of the essential aspects of the prayer's traditional format. He also said praying the Luminous Mysteries should be "left to the freedom of individuals and communities."[13]

At the same time, John Paul II was *inviting* us to join him in reflecting on Christ's public ministry in the rosary. And this is an attractive invitation that makes a lot of sense. As some have noted, in the traditional format of the rosary, the transition from the fifth Joyful Mystery to the first Sorrowful Mystery seemed rather abrupt. We moved from Jesus as a twelve-year-old boy found by his parents in the temple to

Jesus as a thirty-three-year-old man about to be crucified on Calvary, while completely skipping over Christ's public ministry. The Mysteries of Light bridge that gap. John Paul II explains, "To bring out fully the Christological depth of the Rosary it would be suitable to make an addition to the traditional pattern which ... could broaden it to include the mysteries of Christ's public ministry between his Baptism and his passion."[14]

Finally, the pope says the new mysteries will give this prayer "fresh life" at a time when the rosary is devalued in many parts of the Church. He hopes this new vitality will help "enkindle renewed interest in the Rosary's place within Christian spirituality as a true doorway to the depths of the Heart of Christ, ocean of joy and of light, of suffering and of glory."[15] As such, the Mysteries of Light seem to be not only a most fitting development of the rosary but also a providential one for our age, and one that is likely to stand the test of time.

TWO

Discovering the Rosary's Soul: Ten Practical Insights for Greater Devotion

From secular news reports on CNN to jubilant announcements on Catholic websites, much of the immediate reaction to John Paul II's apostolic letter on the rosary centered on the new Mysteries of Light he recommended for our reflection. Since it is rather extraordinary that a pope would add a new set of mysteries to the rosary, one can understand why many gravitated toward this exciting development in Marian devotion unfolding before our eyes.

Little, however, was being said about the rest of the document, which is perhaps just as fascinating. John Paul II shared his heart with the world in this letter and offered a powerful, personal reflection on the importance of the rosary in his own life. In this chapter we will consider several practical insights he offered to help Christians experience the strength and joy that he has found in the daily rhythm of the rosary.

Rediscovering the Rosary's Soul

John Paul II encourages us not to neglect the rosary's *soul*. Like Paul VI, he reminds us that reciting the Our Fathers, Hail Marys, and Glory Bes of the rosary is not an end in itself but a means to a deeper purpose: contemplation of Christ's life.

Yet for many devotees of the rosary, focusing attention on the mysteries can be quite challenging. Despite our best intentions, we find ourselves easily distracted. No matter how much we intend to reflect on the mysteries, our minds somehow end up on other random thoughts: problems at work, projects to get done at home, the movie we saw last night, what shoes we will wear tomorrow, the pizza we'll eat as soon as we're done praying. At the end of the rosary we may feel as if we just rattled off a bunch of prayers while our hearts remained far from the mysteries of Christ.

At other times, we may—much to our embarrassment—treat the rosary as a spiritual chore. We may feel anxious for the task to be completed. A decade can really feel like ten years: "How many beads are left?... We're only on the *second* mystery?"

And at other times we're just plain tired. When finally given a moment to sit down in quiet, we find ourselves struggling to stay awake and falling asleep right in the middle of a Hail Mary.

Whatever struggles we may face with the rosary, we should never walk away from this devotion feeling defeated. The prayers themselves are scriptural and holy, and bringing ourselves to pray the rosary in itself can bear spiritual fruit.

At the same time, John Paul II offers several suggestions to help us enter more profoundly into the mysteries so that the rosary can serve as an even greater source of strength and guidance for our daily lives. Let us consider ten of those insights.

1. Announce Each Mystery and Visualize It

For John Paul II, the crucial moment of the rosary comes before we pray a single Our Father, Hail Mary, or Glory Be. He recommends that at the start of each decade we pause to prepare our minds to reflect on that decade's particular mystery from Christ's life. This is an important first step, for our preparation can set the tone for the entire decade. It can help determine whether the following ten Hail Marys will be a dry, mechanical repetition of formulas or a pathway to communion with Christ.

After announcing the mystery at the beginning of each decade, the pope encourages us to use our imaginations "to open up a scenario on which to focus our attention."[1] One way of concentrating our attention may be to look at an icon that portrays the mystery. Another approach the pope suggests is the Ignatian method of prayer. St. Ignatius of Loyola recommended that Christians use their minds and imaginations to place themselves reflectively in the scene that is being contemplated.

For example, when praying the first Joyful Mystery, the Annunciation, we might imagine what it would have been like to be in the Virgin Mary's home when the angel appeared to her in Nazareth. We can picture the young Mary, perhaps alone in a room praying or doing some work around the house. Suddenly an angel of the Lord appears to her. What does the angel look like? What is Mary's first reaction? What is the look on her face?

We listen to the angel assure her not to be afraid and then announce that she is to become the mother of Israel's messiah. The Jews had been waiting hundreds of years for God to send them the messiah and free them from their sufferings, and now Mary learns that she is the one who will give birth to this king. Even more astonishing is the fact that she will conceive this child not through natural means but as a virgin by the power of God's Spirit!

A lot is being asked of this young woman from Nazareth. How will she respond? Is she afraid? We wait for her answer. Then we picture her, with total trust, saying to the Lord's messenger, "Let it be done unto me according to your word." Now the God of the universe will become a baby in her womb.

This Ignatian method of visualizing biblical scenes also invites us to use our senses during our contemplation. We can imagine the sights, sounds, and smells of each scene as if we were there, too. Applying this method, let us consider the second Luminous Mystery, the wedding at Cana.

Imagine being in a small Galilean village for a first-century Jewish wedding feast. We picture ourselves arriving at a joyful celebration. As we move through the crowd, we hear a lot of music, singing, laughter, and conversation. We smell the aroma coming from the many tables of food. We see the bride and groom smiling and laughing with their families. We also see Mary, Jesus, and some of his disciples enjoying the festivities.

Amid this great feast, we happen to see Mary with a troubled look on her face as she speaks with a few of the servants. She then rushes over to Jesus. There is a mini-crisis, but no one else seems to notice. Mary informs Jesus that the party has run out of wine. What will Jesus do? What *can* he do? Will he send his disciples to get more wine? Will he make wine appear out of nowhere? Mary tells the servants to do whatever her son tells them.

Surprisingly, Jesus simply commands the servants to fill the ritual purification jars with water and serve it to the people. "How will *this* solve the problem?" we wonder. The servants perhaps think this is some practical joke: Have the people drunk so much wine that they won't even notice that water is now being served?

We stay to watch how this "wine" will go over with the steward of the feast. He takes a drink from the jars, and we are shocked to see him smile at the taste of it and hear him praise the bridegroom for serving such great wine: "Every man serves the good wine first; and when men have drunk freely, then the poor wine; but you have kept the good wine until now" (Jn 2:10).

We now taste the wine for ourselves, and sure enough, it is the best wine we have ever had. We finally realize what has happened: The water was changed into wine. Jesus has just performed the first of his miracles here at the wedding feast in Cana.

Applying our imagination and senses to the biblical scenes of Christ's life is an approach that flows from the mystery of the Incarnation itself. As John Paul II explains, by becoming a man and dwelling among us, God chose to reveal himself to us in a way that appeals to the senses. The pope says, "In Jesus, God wanted to take on human features. It is through his bodily reality that we are led into contact with the mystery of his divinity."[2]

2. Listening to the Word of God

Another way to prepare for our reflection on the mysteries is to read from Sacred Scripture at the beginning of each decade. Depending on the circumstances, such a reading could be long (for example, reading the entire account of the Annunciation) or short (reading only a few lines from the scene).

This is not simply a matter of recalling more information for our meditation but of allowing God to speak to our hearts in a unique way.[3] Since Scripture is the inspired Word of God, contact with these sacred words in itself can be a life-transforming experience. The letter to the Hebrews says, "[T]he word of God is living and active, sharper than any two-edged sword, piercing to the division of soul and spirit, of joints and marrow, and discerning the thoughts and intentions of the heart" (Heb 4:12).

Given the power of Sacred Scripture, the pope encourages us to encounter the living Christ while listening to the inspired Word of God during the rosary. "No other words can ever match the efficacy of the inspired word. As we listen, we are certain that this is the word of

God, spoken for today and spoken 'for me.'"[4]

In harmony with this approach, chapters three through six of this book offer biblical reflections on the twenty mysteries. These reflections uncover the historical context, Old Testament background, and spiritual significance of the biblical scenes related to the mysteries of Christ in the rosary. It is my hope that they will draw readers deeper into God's Word and enrich their contemplation of these mysteries of salvation.

3. Silence

Next John Paul II suggests that we pause in silence and take time to ponder the mystery before beginning the vocal prayers of the Our Father, Hail Mary, and Glory Be. This gives us the opportunity at the start of each decade to reflect on the words from Scripture and allow them to soak into our souls.

In a society dominated by technology and mass media, interior silence can be difficult to find. Images from television, movies, and web pages race across our minds and compete for our attention, while sounds from the radio or our favorite CD fill our heads. Our society is afraid of silence. Yet it is in silence that God speaks to our hearts (*CCC*, 2717). John Paul II challenges us to rest in that silence, even briefly, at the start of each decade, so that we might be more open to God's speaking to our hearts in the rosary.

One helpful method for entering into that silence is to focus on one word from the biblical account representing the mystery. Another is to picture just one image from the mystery being contemplated. If given attention, this moment of silence can help settle the soul, calm our scattered thoughts, and direct our attention to God in preparation for the next ten beads.

4. The Our Father: Praying in Union With God's Family

After focusing on the mystery, we begin our vocal prayers by lifting our minds to God the Father. In reciting the Our Father, we express two amazing truths about the Christian life.

First, because of our union with Christ, we truly can call God *Abba*—a term of intimate affection that Jewish children used to address their dads (see Rom 8:15; Gal 4:6).[5] Despite our own weaknesses and repeated failings, God has forgiven our sins, and we can approach him with confidence. We can call him, "Abba." By starting each decade of the rosary with this prayer, we begin our reflection on the life of the Son in union with the gaze from his own Father in heaven.

Secondly, the Our Father expresses our unity with all other Christians. Jesus does not tell us to call God simply "*My* Father" but "*Our* Father." This subtle first word of the Lord's Prayer reminds us that Christianity is not a religion of my own isolated, private relationship with God. Jesus did not come to save us as islands separate from one another. In reconciling us to God, Christ reconciles us to each other. He unites us as brothers and sisters under one Heavenly Father, *Our* Father. Therefore, the Our Father is truly a prayer of the whole family of God, expressing our unity with all our brothers and sisters in Christ throughout the world and throughout time.

Along these lines, John Paul II highlights the profound communal nature of this prayer in the rosary. He explains that the Our Father recited at the start of each decade "makes meditation upon the mystery, even when carried out in solitude, an ecclesial experience"—an experience of the whole Church.[6] In this sense we can say that we never pray the rosary in isolation. Whether we are praying it at home, in a car, on a business trip, in the hospital, or in a nursing home, the Our Fathers underscore the fact that we pray in union with our friends, our family, our fellow Christians here on earth, and even the saints in heaven.

When we pray the rosary, it is as if we are gathered in our Father's arms with all our brothers and sisters throughout the ages to look at "pictures" from the life of our eldest brother, Jesus. In this spiritual family album we remember and celebrate the key moments of Christ's life—the announcement of his birth in Nazareth, his being born in Bethlehem, his ministry in Galilee, his death and resurrection in Jerusalem, and his ascension into heaven. Over and over again, these images of salvation pass before the eyes of our souls as we pray and ponder with his mother, Mary.

5. The Ten Hail Marys: Contemplating Christ With His Mother

In the last chapter we considered how the Hail Mary truly is a Christ-centered prayer. In the first part of this prayer we repeat Gabriel and Elizabeth's joyful response to the mystery of God becoming man in Mary's womb: "Hail Mary, full of grace, the Lord is with thee. Blessed art thou among women and blessed is the fruit of thy womb." Thus in each Hail Mary we have the opportunity to participate in this awe-filled wonder over Jesus while reflecting on the mysteries of salvation in each decade.

John Paul II also reminds us that the "center of gravity" for the Hail Mary is Christ's holy name: "And blessed is the fruit of thy womb, *Jesus.*" He encourages us not to recite the Hail Mary too quickly, but to reverence the name of Jesus each time it is spoken in this prayer: "Sometimes, in a hurried recitation, this center of gravity can be overlooked, and with it the connection to the mystery of Christ being contemplated. Yet it is precisely the emphasis given to the name of Jesus and to his mystery that is the sign of a meaningful and fruitful recitation of the Rosary."[7]

The pope offers one suggestion on how we can give special attention to Christ's name in the rosary. After saying Jesus' name in each

Hail Mary, we can add a clause related to the mystery being contemplated. For example, in the first sorrowful mystery (the agony in the garden), one could say, "Blessed art thou among women, and blessed is the fruit of thy womb, *Jesus, agonizing in the garden.*" In the fifth glorious mystery (the crowning of Mary), one could pray, "Blessed art thou among women and blessed is the fruit of thy womb, Jesus, *who crowned you as queen of heaven and earth.*" In the third luminous mystery (the proclamation of the kingdom), one could say with each Hail Mary, "... and blessed is the fruit of thy womb, Jesus, *who calls us to conversion.*"

John Paul II says this popular practice, which was spread by St. Louis de Montfort and others, "gives forceful expression to our faith in Christ, directed to the different moments of the Redeemer's life. It is at once *a profession of faith* and an aid in concentrating our meditation, since it facilitates the process of assimilation to the mystery of Christ inherent in the repetition of the *Hail Mary.*"[8]

In the last part of this prayer we ask Mary to intercede for us as we ponder the mysteries of Christ. John Paul II explains that contemplation is simply looking upon the face of Jesus. Since no one has devoted themselves to this loving task more than Christ's mother, it makes sense that Christians would want to gaze upon the face of Jesus in union with her.

He says, "In a unique way the face of the Son belongs to Mary. It was in her womb that Christ was formed, receiving from her a human resemblance that points to an even greater spiritual closeness.... The eyes of her heart already turned to him at the Annunciation, when she conceived him by the power of the Holy Spirit. In the months that followed she began to sense his presence and to picture his features. When at last she gave birth to him in Bethlehem, her eyes were able to gaze tenderly on the face of her Son, as she 'wrapped him in swaddling clothes, and laid him in a manger' (Lk 2:7). Therefore, Mary's gaze, ever filled with adoration and wonder would never leave him."[9]

John Paul II goes on to note how Mary was with Jesus at his first miracle at Cana, where she anticipated his desire to change the water into wine (see Jn 2:4). She watched her son die on the cross, but her sorrow turned to radiant joy when she witnessed his resurrection on Easter (see Acts 1:14). As the pope explains, "no one knows Christ better than Mary; no one can introduce us to a profound knowledge of his mystery better than his Mother."[10]

This is why it is fitting to ask for Our Lady's intercession as we reflect on Christ's birth, life, death, and resurrection in the rosary. No one has contemplated his life more than Mary. "Contemplating the scenes of the Rosary in union with Mary is a means of learning from her to 'read' Christ, to discover his secrets and to understand his message."[11] She can draw us more deeply into Christ through her loving prayers for us—both "now" as we pray the rosary and "at the hour of our death."

6. The Glory Be: The Height of Our Contemplation

Glory be to the Father, and to the Son, and to the Holy Spirit, as it was in the beginning, is now and ever shall be, world without end. Amen.

This short prayer of praise known as the "Glory Be" comes at the end of each decade, but it is not simply a closing prayer. Rather it is meant to express the peak of our contemplation.

Praise of the Holy Trinity is the Christian response to the events of salvation that God has accomplished in his Son. We praise God for his becoming man and dwelling among us, for his death which conquered sin, for his resurrection which gives us new life, for his ascension to the right hand of the Father, and for sending the Holy Spirit to us at Pentecost (*CCC*, 2641).

John Paul II says, "To the extent that meditation on the mystery is attentive and profound, and to the extent that it is enlivened—from one *Hail Mary* to another—by love for Christ and for Mary, the glorification of the Trinity at the end of each decade, far from being a perfunctory conclusion, takes on its proper contemplative tone, raising the mind as it were to the heights of heaven, and enabling us in some way to relive the experience of [the Transfiguration], a foretaste of the contemplation yet to come: 'It is good for us to be here!' (Lk 9:33)."[12]

In other words, when we attentively ponder the mysteries of salvation in the rosary, we cannot help but cry out in praise and thanksgiving, "Glory be to the Father, and to the Son, and to the Holy Spirit!" This is why John Paul II says the Glory Be should be given due importance in the rosary. He even suggests that when the rosary is recited publicly, this prayer of praise could be sung.

7. A Concluding Prayer: Life Application

It is common to say a brief prayer after each Glory Be. One popular practice is to recite the "Fatima prayer": "O my Jesus, forgive us our sins, save us from the fires of hell, lead all souls to heaven, especially those in most need of thy mercy." In the reported apparition of Mary to three children in Fatima, Portugal, in 1917, she asked that this prayer be recited at the end of each decade.

John Paul II leaves open other possibilities for prayers at the close of each decade, in harmony with local customs and diverse traditions. However, he suggests that contemplation of the mysteries could be expressed more fully "with a prayer for the fruits specific to that particular mystery."[13] For example, at the end of the first joyful mystery (the Annunciation), we could say, "Pray for us, Mary, that we may respond in obedient faith each day as you did." Or after the fourth sorrowful mystery (the carrying of the cross), we could say, "Pray for us,

Mary, that we may carry our daily crosses in union with your son, Jesus." Or after the first glorious mystery (the Resurrection), we could say, "Pray for us, Mary, that we would share the peace of the Risen Christ with those around us."

The pope hopes that this practice will help connect the rosary even more with our daily life as Christians.

8. The Beads as Symbols

John Paul II notes how even the rosary beads can play an important part in our devotion. On one hand, the beads liberate the mind from worrying about counting each Hail Mary. On the other hand, the beads themselves take on a symbolism that can be helpful for contemplation.

First, he points out, all the beads converge on the crucifix, which represents the beginning and end point of the rosary's prayers. This can remind us how the entire Christian life is centered on Christ: "Everything begins from him, everything leads toward him, everything, through him, in the Holy Spirit, attains to the Father."[14]

Second, the pope notes that the beads symbolize a chain linking us to God as his servants. This is "a sweet chain" that is joined by the bonds of love. Our contemplation of Christ in the rosary can help draw us out of ourselves, out of our slavery to sin, and out of whatever addictions may keep us from living more fully with Christ. Perhaps we struggle with traditional addictions to alcohol, pornography, sexual pleasure, or work. Or maybe we suffer from more subtle addictions to compliments, to pleasing everyone, to being the center of attention, or to being in control. The "sweet chain" of the rosary can free us from these fatal attractions by bringing our hearts into contact with something much more alluring: the infinite love of Jesus Christ.[15]

Third, the linking of the many rosary beads joined at the crucifix reminds us of our many relationships—family, friends, coworkers, neighbors, fellow Christians, the saints, and the angels—that are all intertwined in the common bond of Christ. When we pray the rosary, we can take time to pray for all these relationships, either in our hearts or by offering prayer intentions before we begin.

9. Opening and Closing

In different parts of the Church there are diverse ways of introducing the rosary. One widely followed practice is to recite the Creed, one Our Father, three Hail Marys, and a Glory Be as a prelude to the decades. This custom and others are intended to prepare the mind for contemplation of the mysteries.

At the end of the rosary we pray for the intentions of the pope, embracing the needs of the Church as a whole. One common practice is to recite an Our Father, Hail Mary, and Glory Be for the Holy Father's intentions for the Church and for the world. Finally, we recite a concluding prayer, such as the Hail Holy Queen or the Litany of Mary, in thanksgiving for Mary's intercession for us throughout our contemplation of Christ in the rosary. John Paul II calls this a most fitting conclusion:

"Is it any wonder, then, that the soul feels the need, after saying this prayer and experiencing so profoundly the motherhood of Mary, to burst forth into praise of the Blessed Virgin, either in that splendid prayer the *Salve Regina* [Hail Holy Queen] or in the *Litany of Loreto?* This is the crowning moment of an inner journey which has brought the faithful into living contact with the mystery of Christ and his Blessed Mother."[16]

10. The Weekly Rhythm of the Mysteries

Technically speaking, the rosary itself consists of twenty decades in which all four sets of mysteries are contemplated: the Joyful, Luminous, Sorrowful, and Glorious. The pope notes that the full rosary can be recited every day by contemplative priests and religious and by the sick and elderly, who often have more time at their disposal. However, since most people will be able to recite only part of the rosary each day, he recommends that we dedicate different days of the week to different sets of mysteries.

In previous practice, Monday and Thursday were dedicated to the Joyful Mysteries; Tuesday and Friday to the Sorrowful Mysteries; and Sunday, Wednesday, and Saturday to the Glorious Mysteries. With the introduction of the Mysteries of Light, John Paul II proposes a new weekly pattern.

He recommends that, since Saturday traditionally is associated with Mary, the Joyful Mysteries (in which Mary's presence is stressed more than in any other set of mysteries) be prayed on Saturday and Monday instead of Thursday and Monday. This would free Thursday for the Mysteries of Light—a fitting day for these mysteries since they culminate with the Institution of the Eucharist, which is celebrated on Holy Thursday in the Church's liturgical calendar.

Thus, while being open to other possibilities for distributing the mysteries, depending on particular pastoral needs, the pope proposes this new weekly schedule for the Church:

Monday:	Joyful Mysteries
Tuesday:	Sorrowful Mysteries
Wednesday:	Glorious Mysteries
Thursday:	Luminous Mysteries
Friday:	Sorrowful Mysteries
Saturday:	Joyful Mysteries
Sunday:	Glorious Mysteries

By reflecting on different mysteries throughout the week, the rosary gives each day its own "spiritual color," like the liturgical colors that accent the different seasons of the Church's year. Week after week we ponder anew the key moments in Christ's life—his birth, public ministry, death, and resurrection—and in these mysteries we find the meaning of our own life's story, from birth to death, from joy to sorrow, from suffering to triumph, and ultimately, from this pilgrimage on earth to our hope in everlasting life. In this way the rosary does indeed, as John Paul II says, "mark the rhythm of human life, bringing it into harmony with the 'rhythm' of God's own life."[17]

THREE

Scriptural Reflections on the Joyful Mysteries

John Paul II says the Joyful Mysteries "are marked by the joy radiating from the event of the Incarnation."[1] We first see this joy in Gabriel's greeting of Mary, as the God of the universe is about to enter the human family in her womb. In the visitation John the Baptist leaps for joy before the presence of Christ in Mary. In the nativity the angels proclaim the "good news of a great joy" (Lk 2:10) to the shepherds who encounter the newborn Savior in Bethlehem.

John Paul II notes that the final two mysteries include a "joy mixed with drama," as they foreshadow the sorrow of Christ's suffering and death. In the presentation the elderly Simeon rejoices in finally holding the Messiah in his arms. But he also foretells how the child will face intense opposition as an adult and how Mary will suffer greatly when her son is killed. The last joyful mystery presents the twelve-year-old Christ going to Jerusalem for Passover and being lost for three days while doing his Father's will. This foreshadows his return to Jerusalem for Passover as an adult and his being "lost" when he is crucified on the cross, doing the will of his Father. As in his youth, Christ will be found again on the third day—this time in his resurrection.

The First Joyful Mystery:
The Annunciation
Luke 1:26-38

In the sixth month the angel Gabriel was sent from God to a city of Galilee named Nazareth, to a virgin betrothed to a man whose name was Joseph, of the house of David; and the virgin's name was Mary. And he came to her and said, "Hail, full of grace, the Lord is with you!"

LUKE 1:26-28

The mystery of Christ begins in the quiet life of one young Jewish woman who from all outward appearances seems to be rather ordinary. She is a virgin betrothed to a man named Joseph, and she is probably in her early teen years. She lives in a small, insignificant village called Nazareth. Her name is Mary.

Suddenly, in the midst of her simple, routine life in Nazareth, an amazing event occurs: An angel of the Lord appears to her and says, "Hail, full of grace, the Lord is with you!" (Lk 1:28).

No angel has ever greeted anyone with such exalted language. Gabriel addresses Mary not by her personal name but with a title, "full of grace." As John Paul II comments, "'Full of grace' is the name Mary possesses in the eyes of God."[2]

In Greek the word commonly translated "full of grace" (*kecharito-mene*) indicates that Mary already was filled with God's saving grace. Chosen from the beginning of time to be the mother of the Savior, Mary has been prepared by God to be a pure, spotless sanctuary in which his Son would dwell. Now the all-holy Son of God will enter the world through the womb of a woman who is "full of grace."

The Lord Is With You!

The angel then says, "The Lord is with you!" For many Catholics these words might seem like a routine response said at Mass. However, for a Jewish woman of Mary's times, hearing "The Lord is with you!" would signal that she is called to play a crucial role in God's plan of salvation.

In the Old Testament this phrase often was used when someone was being called for a special mission. For example, when Moses was called to lead the people out of Egypt, God told him, "I will be with you." When Joshua was called to lead Israel into the Promised Land, God said to him, "I will be with you." When Gideon was called to defend the people against the Philistines, when David was called to lead the kingdom, when Jeremiah the prophet was called to challenge the rulers in Jerusalem, they were all told that the Lord would be with them.

In each case the person was commissioned to take on a difficult task with many risks and challenges. Often they felt inadequate and ill-prepared. Nevertheless, God challenged them to step outside their "comfort zones" and rely on him as never before. While they may not have felt ready for the job, they were given the one thing they needed most to carry out their task: The Lord would be with them.

Mary is about to be given one of the most important missions in Israel's history: to be the mother of the Messiah, who will bring salvation to the whole world. Such a role will not be easy. It will take her through many periods of trial, uncertainty, confusion, and suffering. Nevertheless, Gabriel tells Mary that she has the one thing she needs to be faithful to God's plan: The Lord is with her.

Mother of the King

"And behold, you will conceive in your womb and bear a son, and you shall call his name Jesus. He will be great, and will be called the Son of the Most High; and the Lord God will give to him the throne of his father David, and he will reign over the house of Jacob for ever; and of his kingdom there will be no end" (Lk 1:31-33).

Gabriel's message recalls the covenant promises God made to King David. In 2 Samuel 7, God told David that he would make his name "great" and establish "the throne of his kingdom for ever." David's royal descendants would be like God's son, and his "house" and "kingdom" "shall be made sure for ever" (2 Sm 7:9-16).

For centuries, however, this Davidic dynasty stood in ruins. From the sixth century B.C. to Mary's time, practically, one foreign nation after another dominated the Jewish land, and no Davidic king ruled on the throne. Through the prophets, God promised the Jews that he would send them a new king who would free them from their enemies and fulfill the promises he made to David. This king would be called the Messiah, the "anointed one." In Mary's day the Jews were still waiting and wondering when God would send the Messiah to rescue them.

It is within this context that Gabriel tells Mary she will have a son to whom the Lord will give "the throne of his father David." And this son "will reign over the house of Jacob for ever; and of his kingdom there will be no end." Echoing the promises God made to David, Gabriel announces the arrival of the everlasting kingdom with this child.

Imagine how Mary must have felt when she realized that the Messiah-King was finally coming to Israel—and that *she* was chosen to be his mother! In her womb she would carry all of Israel's deepest hopes and longings.

Conceived by the Holy Spirit

But how would this conception take place? Mary is a virgin and is not yet living with Joseph. She asks the angel, "How can this be, since I have no husband?" (Lk 1:34).

Now Gabriel delivers the most breathtaking part of his message: Mary will not have this child through natural means. No, miraculously, as a virgin, she will conceive through the power of God's Holy Spirit. Thus this child will not only be the messianic son of David; he will be the divine Son of God coming from the Spirit and power of God himself: "The Holy Spirit will come upon you, and the power of the Most High will overshadow you; therefore the child to be born will be called holy, the Son of God" (Lk 1:35).

What a mystery! The God of the entire universe will dwell in the virgin's womb. Mary will give birth to the One who gave her life. She will raise the child who is her own savior. The Church's liturgical prayer expresses this mystery very well by referring to Mary as "Mother of her creator" and addressing her with the paradoxical title "daughter of your Son."[3]

Mary's "Yes"

God is asking a lot of Mary. Consider all that has taken place in this brief encounter with Gabriel. First she is told that she will be expecting a child. Next she learns that this child will be Israel's long-awaited Messiah. Then she discovers that her child will be the divine Son of God. And finally she is told that she will conceive of this child as a virgin through the Holy Spirit of God. This is an awful lot to swallow in one short conversation with an angel!

What does this all mean? Where will this lead her? Does she feel ready to be a mother and, even more, ready to be the mother of God? What will Joseph think when he finds out that she is pregnant? A lot of questions could have been racing through her mind.

According to St. Bernard of Clairvaux and others, all the angels and saints of the Old Testament would have been holding their breaths at this moment, wondering how the virgin would respond. Whatever she might have been thinking, the one thing we know for sure about Mary's reaction to God's extraordinary calling for her is that she had total trust. She says, "Behold, I am the handmaid of the Lord; let it be to me according to your word" (Lk 1:38).

John Paul II pointed out that Mary's language ("let it be to me") indicates not a passive acceptance but an active embracing of God's plan for her.[4] Her words imply a wish or desire for God's will in her life. As such, Mary's "yes" serves as a model of faith for all believers.

We Christians sometimes submit to the Lord's will begrudgingly, as if it were something burdensome—a sacrifice we must make for the kingdom of God. ("I pray each day because *God* wants me to." "I am kind to that annoying person because, as a Christian, I *have* to do that." "I fast in Lent because *the Church* tells me to.") However, as we grow as God's children, we begin to realize that his plan for our lives always corresponds to our heart's deepest longings, to what will truly bring us fulfillment. Though at times very demanding and involving great sacrifices, God's will is not simply an ethical test we must pass or an external code of behavior to which we must submit. Ultimately, God's will is written on our hearts and is meant to lead us to a profound peace and happiness, even in the face of trials and sufferings.

May we, like Mary, actively desire God's will to be fulfilled in our lives. May we joyfully embrace his plan for us, not simply as a religious rule to obey but ultimately, as the divine pathway to our hearts' deepest and most noble desires.

The Second Joyful Mystery:
The Visitation
Luke 1:39-56

In those days Mary arose and went with haste into the hill country, to a city of Judah, and she entered the house of Zechariah and greeted Elizabeth. And when Elizabeth heard the greeting of Mary, the babe leaped in her womb; and Elizabeth was filled with the Holy Spirit and she exclaimed with a loud cry, "Blessed are you among women, and blessed is the fruit of your womb! And why is this granted me, that the mother of my Lord should come to me?"

LUKE 1:39-43

Elizabeth has been barren all her life, but in the Annunciation Mary has learned that her kinswoman is miraculously expecting a child in her old age, "For with God nothing will be impossible" (Lk 1:37). Upon hearing this good news, Mary fervently desires to share in Elizabeth's joy and serve her during the last part of the pregnancy. She goes "with haste" to visit Elizabeth and then remains with her for three months.

Imagine the meeting of these two expectant mothers. What joy and excitement they must have had for each other. Elizabeth rushes out to greet Mary, saying, "Blessed are you among women, and blessed is the fruit of your womb!" (Lk 1:42). Filled with the Holy Spirit, Elizabeth recognizes that of all the women who have ever lived, Mary is most blessed, for the child in her womb is not any ordinary son but the Son of God himself.

In awe over this mystery, Elizabeth feels a bit unworthy to be in the presence of the Lord dwelling in Mary. She says, "why is this granted me, that the mother of my Lord should come to me?" Even the baby John the Baptist recognizes the presence of Jesus, leaping in Elizabeth's womb as soon as Mary arrives.

Mary, Ark of the Covenant

This joy-filled reception of Mary and Jesus in the Visitation is reminiscent of the way the ark of the covenant was welcomed in the Old Testament. As Israel's most important religious vessel, the ark carried three sacred items: the Ten Commandments; the staff of Aaron (the first high priest); and a jar containing *manna* (the heavenly bread that fed the Israelites for forty years in the desert) (see Heb 9:4). Yet what made the ark most holy was God's presence, which overshadowed it in the form of a cloud that filled the sanctuary.

When David became king, he wanted the ark to be brought to his capital city of Jerusalem. On the way there the ark took a journey that is important for understanding the visitation scene. First the ark traveled to *the hill country of Judea*, and it remained there in the *house of Obededom* for *three months* (see 2 Sm 6:2, 11). When it eventually arrived in Jerusalem, there was a grand procession, with people *shouting* joyfully before the ark and David *leaping* before the Lord's presence (see 2 Sm 6:12-16). The account also mentions that David's initial response to the ark was one of fear and wonder: "*How can the ark of the Lord come to me?*" (2 Sm 6:9).

All this prefigures Mary's journey to visit Elizabeth. Like the ark of the covenant, Mary also travels "to the hill country ... of Judea" and remains in a family's house, the "house of Zechariah," for "three months" (Lk 1:39-40, 56). Like David leaping before the ark, John the Baptist "leaped" in his mother's womb before Mary (Lk 1:41). And similar to David's awe-filled response before the ark of the covenant, Elizabeth says to Mary, "And why is this granted me, that the mother of my Lord should come to me?" (Lk 1:43).

Finally, like the ark, Mary is greeted with shouts of joy, as Elizabeth "exclaimed with a loud cry" (Lk 1:42). The particular word Luke uses for "exclaimed" is found only five times in the entire Old Testament. In every case it refers to people exclaiming and praising God *before the ark of the covenant.* Elizabeth exclaiming before Mary is thus reminiscent of the Jewish priests exclaiming God's praises before the ark of the Lord.

These extensive parallels demonstrate clearly that Luke is presenting Mary as a new ark of the covenant. What does this mean?

Just as God's presence once overshadowed the sanctuary, which housed the ark, so does the Holy Spirit now overshadow Mary (see Ex 40:34-35; Lk 1:35). As the ark carried the Ten Commandments, so does Mary carry in her womb the one who has come to fulfill the Law (see Mt 5:17). As the ark carried the staff of the first high priest, so does Mary carry within her the last and true high priest, who will offer the perfect sacrifice to redeem the world (see Heb 8:1-7). As the ark carried the heavenly bread called manna, so does Mary bear Jesus, who will call himself the *true* Bread of Life come down from heaven (see Jn 6:48-51).

Most of all, as the ark of old bore God's presence to Israel, Mary bears the presence of God become man to the whole world. And as the new ark of the covenant, she continues her role of bringing Christ into the world today through her powerful intercession for our lives.

The *Magnificat*

What is going on inside Mary in these days after the Annunciation? She certainly has had a lot of time to reflect on her profound vocation to serve as the mother of the world's Savior. During her long journey to Elizabeth's village, she probably pondered in her heart over and over again the words Gabriel spoke to her. And all the way to Judea she knew she was no longer alone. She now carries in her womb the Son of God.

In the Visitation scene Mary breaks out into a hymn-like praise of

God: "My soul magnifies the Lord, and my spirit rejoices in God my Savior, for he has regarded the low estate of his handmaiden. For behold, henceforth all generations will call me blessed; for he who is mighty has done great things for me, and holy is his name. And his mercy is on those who fear him from generation to generation" (Lk 1:46-50).

This praise, commonly known as the *Magnificat*, tells us something about the *interior* journey Mary has been making. John Paul II says it represents the hidden depths of Mary's faith in these days.[5]

First Mary thanks the mighty God who has "done great things" for her. Viewing herself as a lowly servant, Mary humbly stands in awe before the fact that God has chosen her for such a high calling as to serve as the mother of the Messiah.

However, in the second half of the *Magnificat*, Mary sees a connection between what God has done for her and what God wants to accomplish in the lives of all his people. She will bear the son who will do great things for *all* the lowly in Israel and in the world:

"He has shown strength with his arm, he has scattered the proud in the imagination of their hearts, he has put down the mighty from their thrones, and exalted those of low degree; he has filled the hungry with good things, and the rich he has sent empty away. He has helped his servant Israel, in remembrance of his mercy, as he spoke to our fathers, to Abraham and to his posterity for ever" (Lk 1:51-55).

Here Mary views herself as the first recipient of the blessings God wishes to bring to all the faithful. Just as the Lord raised up Mary from her own lowliness because she was a faithful servant, God wishes to exalt all the lowly and show mercy to all who fear him. Just as God has shown favor to his handmaiden Mary, so he will help "his servant Israel."

The *Magnificat* thus tells us that what God has done for this lowly woman of Nazareth, he will do for all who humbly serve him as Mary did. God will bless our faithfulness, look mercifully on our lowliness, and exalt us in our afflictions. May we imitate Mary in thanking and praising the mighty God, who does "great things" for us. May we forever sing with her, "My soul magnifies the Lord!"

The Third Joyful Mystery:
The Nativity
Luke 2:1-20

In those days a decree went out from Caesar Augustus that all the world should be enrolled.... And all went to be enrolled, each to his own city. And Joseph also went up from Galilee, from the city of Nazareth, to Judea, to the city of David, which is called Bethlehem, because he was of the house and lineage of David, to be enrolled with Mary his betrothed, who was with child. And while they were there, the time came for her to be delivered. And she gave birth to her first-born son and wrapped him in swaddling cloths, and laid him in a manger, because there was no place for them in the inn.

Luke 2:1, 3-7

The son of God enters the world with much hardship and poverty. While Mary is in the last months of her pregnancy, she and Joseph are uprooted from their home in Nazareth and forced to travel to Bethlehem to be counted in a census—an oppressive tool that the Romans used to help them collect taxes from the people. Because "there was no place for them in the inn" (Lk 2:7), Mary experiences childbirth in an environment of extreme poverty. She cannot even give

Jesus the basics of what any mother would want to offer a newborn baby. Instead a manger, a feeding trough for the animals, serves as an improvised cradle for the Son of God.[6]

Some early Christians saw Christ's humble beginnings in a manger as a foreshadowing of how he continues to meet us in the Eucharist. For example, St. Cyril of Alexandria said that when we sin, we fail to live out our dignity as humans made in the image of God, and we instead become like animals, living a life of self-gratification. Yet while animals feed from an ordinary manger, we as sinners approach Christ in a feeding trough that is much more substantial. Jesus feeds us not with hay but with his own Body and Blood in the Eucharist.[7] Along these lines, it is interesting to note that Jesus, the Eucharistic "bread of life" (Jn 6:35), is born in the city of Bethlehem, which in Hebrew literally means "house of bread."

The Glory of the Lord

"And in that region there were shepherds out in the field, keeping watch over their flock by night. And an angel of the Lord appeared to them, and the glory of the Lord shone around them, and they were filled with fear" (Lk 2:8-9).

In the fields a group of shepherds are tending their flock by night, unaware of the Savior child who has just been born in the city nearby. Suddenly their ordinary lives are dramatically disrupted. Out of the darkness comes a dazzling brightness that encircles them, and they are afraid. It is "the glory of the Lord."

What is this glory that the shepherds behold? In the Old Testament God's "glory" was the visible manifestation of his divine presence. It often came in the form of a cloud, covering the ark of the covenant or filling the temple in Jerusalem (see Ex 40:34; 1 Kgs 8:11; Ez 10:4, 18). When the prophet Ezekiel had a vision of God's glory in the temple, he fell on his face in worship (see Ez 44:4).

The glory of the Lord, however, did not remain in the land of Israel forever. Shortly before Babylon invaded Jerusalem and destroyed the temple in 586 B.C., God's glory left the sanctuary and the holy city because of the people's sinfulness (see Ez 10–11). For hundreds of years the Jewish people were without God's glory dwelling among them—until this night of Christ's birth. The same divine glory that once hovered over the ark of the covenant and filled the Holy of Holies now envelops these simple shepherds in an open field outside Bethlehem.

Amid the brightness an angel appears and assures them: "Be not afraid; for behold, I bring you good news of a great joy which will come to all the people; for to you is born this day in the city of David a Savior, who is Christ the Lord" (Lk 2:10-11).

Then a countless number of angels appear from heaven, praising God and saying, "Glory to God in the highest, and on earth peace among men with whom he is pleased!" (Lk 2:14). In their hymn of praise over the Bethlehem fields these heavenly representatives joyfully recognize what seems to have gone unnoticed by almost everyone on earth: Today is born the Savior of the world, Christ the Lord!

The Shepherds' Encounter

Shepherds sat at the bottom of the social scale in first-century Judaism. Often working for landowners, they received low wages. Religious Jews considered them dishonest and outside of God's covenant. It is therefore remarkable that God chooses to announce Christ's birth not to the religious leaders in Jerusalem, but to these lowly shepherds in the Bethlehem fields.

And the shepherds respond promptly to God's call. They receive the angel's message with enthusiastic faith, saying, "Let us go over to Bethlehem and see this thing that has happened, which the Lord has made known to us" (Lk 2:15). They rush to the city "with haste" and find what they have been looking for: Mary, Joseph, and the child Jesus lying in a manger, just as the angel told them.

The shepherds marvel at their encounter with the newborn Christ and eagerly desire to tell others about the newborn child (see Lk 2:18). On this first Christmas night they go back to the fields with their lives transformed, echoing the angels' hymn of praise at the birth of Jesus: "And the shepherds returned, glorifying and praising God for all they had heard and seen" (Lk 2:20).

We too share in the angels' joyous announcement whenever we sing the *Gloria* at the beginning of Mass. Just as the angels welcomed the birth of Jesus in Bethlehem, singing "Glory to God," we prepare to welcome his coming in the Eucharist by praising the Lord, saying: "Glory to God in the highest and peace to his people on earth...."

The Fourth Joyful Mystery:
The Presentation
Luke 2:22-40

Mary and Joseph travel to Jerusalem to present Jesus in the temple. According to the Jewish law, the parents of a firstborn son would offer a small payment to the temple priests and return home with their child.

There in the temple Mary and Joseph meet an aged Jewish man, Simeon, who has been waiting his whole life to lay his eyes on the Messiah. In great rejoicing over seeing Jesus, Simeon praises God and blesses the holy family (see Lk 2:29-34).

The family also encounters a female prophet, Anna, who never leaves the temple courts but worships God day and night. She, too, gives thanks to God, talking about him to everyone in the temple (see Lk 2:36-38). The scene concludes with a statement that foreshadows the greatness of the Christ child: "And the child grew and became strong, filled with wisdom; and the favor of God was upon him" (Lk 2:40).

Greater Than Samuel

Luke's account of Jesus' presentation in the temple is reminiscent of one of the most famous dedication scenes in the Old Testament: that of Samuel, who grew up to serve at the founding of the Davidic kingdom.

Like Mary and Joseph, Samuel's parents (Hanna and Elkanah) were devout Israelites who brought their child to the sanctuary and presented him to the Lord's service. They, too, encountered an elderly religious man (Eli) who blessed them (see 1 Sm 2:20). The story of Samuel's beginnings also mentions women ministering outside the sanctuary (see 1 Sm 2:22) and a statement about the growth of the child: "Now the boy Samuel continued to grow both in stature and in favor with the Lord and with men" (1 Sm 2:26).

The parallels suggest that Luke is portraying Jesus as a new servant of the Lord. Just as Samuel was one of Israel's most important priests and prophets because of his key role in building the kingdom of David, so Jesus will go on to serve as the last and greatest of all the priests and prophets in Israel's history, for he will be the one to establish the everlasting kingdom of God.

Great Expectations

"Now there was a man in Jerusalem whose name was Simeon, and this man was righteous and devout, looking for the consolation of Israel, and the Holy Spirit was upon him. And it had been revealed to him by the Holy Spirit that he should not see death before he had seen the Lord's Christ" (Lk 2:25-26).

Simeon is a model Jew. He is righteous and devout, and is waiting for God to rescue his people Israel. Moreover, God has given Simeon a most extraordinary revelation: He will not die until he sees the Messiah. Patiently waiting and yearning to see the face of Christ, Simeon represents the many faithful Jews who for centuries have been longing for God to act in their lives, free them from their sufferings, and send them the Messiah-King.

Then one day it finally happens. Simeon is inspired by the Holy Spirit to visit the temple (see Lk 2:27). A man open to God's action in his life, Simeon responds to the Spirit's prompting. When he arrives at the temple, he encounters Joseph, Mary, and the child. What a moment this must be for Simeon!

He takes the child in his arms and blesses God, saying: "Lord, now lettest thou thy servant depart in peace, according to thy word; for mine eyes have seen thy salvation which thou hast prepared in the presence of all peoples, a light for revelation to the Gentiles, and for glory to thy people Israel" (Lk 2:29-32).

After years of longing for God to act, Simeon can finally go to his rest. He has seen with his own eyes what God does for those who patiently wait on the Lord. He has held in his own arms the hopes of all of Israel. In this child, God has been faithful to his promises and will rescue his people.

A Sword Will Pierce Your Soul Also

The joy radiating throughout this scene suddenly turns to sorrow. After praising God for sending the savior, Simeon turns to Mary and utters the following prophecy: "Behold, this child is set for the fall and rising of many in Israel, and for a sign that is spoken against (and a sword will pierce through your own soul also), that thoughts out of many hearts may be revealed" (Lk 2:34-35).

With these words Mary catches a glimpse of the difficult road that lies ahead. Her son's future will be full of conflict and turmoil. Simeon first says the child "is set for the fall and rising of many in Israel." This foreshadows how many of the poor and the outcasts of Jesus' day will be exalted in his ministry, while many of the Jewish leaders will reject him and exclude themselves from his kingdom. Simeon also says the child will be "a sign that is spoken against," meaning that Jesus will face hostile opposition, even from his own people. Most devastating is the image of the "sword," which signifies bloodshed and death. This points forward to how Jesus eventually will suffer bloodshed on the cross and be killed by his enemies.

A Second Annunication

By saying to Mary "a sword will pierce *through your soul also*," Simeon emphasizes the effects Christ's sufferings will have in her own life. John Paul II says these words represent "a second annunciation" to Mary because they show her more clearly how her initial "yes" to God will be lived out in much suffering. She will see her son misunderstood and plotted against throughout his public ministry, and eventually killed by his enemies in Jerusalem.[8]

Consider the heroic faith of Mary in those dark moments on Good Friday. Gabriel originally told her that she would be the mother of Israel's Messiah, the mother of the One whose kingdom would have no end. Yet as John Paul II points out, at the foot of the cross Mary would be a witness, from a *human* perspective, to the complete negation of those words about Christ's everlasting kingship. Humanly speaking, the cross was anything but royal splendor; it was tragedy and defeat, especially for the mother who could do nothing but helplessly watch her son die such a horrible death.

How great then must have been her trust as she entered what could be called a "spiritual crucifixion," letting go of her son and abandoning herself to God's care in this time of darkness.[9] These trials at Calvary already are foreshadowed in this scene from Christ's infancy with Simeon's prophetic warning to Mary, "A sword will pierce your soul also."

The Fifth Joyful Mystery:
The Finding of the Child Jesus in the Temple
Luke 2:41-52

Supposing him to be in the company they went a day's journey, and they sought him among their kinsfolk and acquaintances; and when they did not find him, they returned to Jerusalem, seeking him.

LUKE 2:44

Imagine what Mary and Joseph are experiencing. When making a pilgrimage to Jerusalem for a feast like Passover, it was common for Jews to travel in large caravans made up of extended family members and friends. Assuming Jesus was with one of their kinsfolk, Mary and Joseph go a whole day's journey without realizing that their child is missing.

But at the end of the day they cannot find him. They search for him frantically throughout the caravan. They ask their friends and relatives. No one has even seen him.

Now they return to Jerusalem. After looking throughout the city, they enter the temple on the third day and find Jesus talking with the

Jewish rabbis, stunning them with his knowledge. Astonished, Mary approaches Jesus and says to him, "Son, why have you treated us so? Behold, your father and I have been looking for you anxiously" (Lk 2:48).

Jesus responds, "How is it that you sought me? Did you not know that I must be in *my Father's house?*" This expression could be translated "my Father's affairs" or "my Father's business" (Lk 2:49). At a young age, Jesus already is emphasizing that he must be busy doing the will of his heavenly Father, even if it means suffering for those he loves. Mary and Joseph, however, are bewildered by their son's statement: "They did not understand the saying which he spoke to them" (Lk 2:50).

A Preview to Good Friday

They lost Jesus. They could not find him for three days. They did not understand. This scene from the childhood of Jesus prefigures what will take place at the climax of his ministry as an adult. In the last days of his life Jesus will make another pilgrimage to Jerusalem for the feast of Passover. There in the holy city he will enter the temple and engage the Jewish teachers in the sanctuary. He will amaze many with his wisdom, just as he did in his youth.

On this occasion, however, the astonishment will lead to his demise as the Jerusalem leaders plot his death. Once again Jesus will be taken away from his mother, this time to be crucified on Calvary. And standing below the cross, Mary, as would any mother, will feel the pains of not fully understanding how her son could suffer such a tragic death. Yet at the same time Mary, through her faith, will trust that Jesus must be about his "Father's house," fulfilling the will of the Father. And just as Mary found Jesus on the third day in Jerusalem as a child, she will find him again *on the third day* when he rises from the dead on Easter morning.

Lost and Found

The Catholic theologian Romano Guardini once said that Mary and Joseph's experience in this scene sometimes repeats itself spiritually in the life of the Christian.

When we first grow in our faith as adults, we may desire Christ deeply in our lives and feel close to him in prayer. But after some time, our spiritual life might become dry, and we may wonder if God is really near us in our prayer. Commenting on these periods of spiritual dryness, Guardini says: "At first, Christ is the center; our faith in Him is firm and loving. But then He disappears for a while, suddenly and apparently without the slightest reason. A remoteness has been created. A void is formed. We feel forsaken. Faith seems folly.... Everything becomes heavy, wearisome, and senseless. We must walk alone and seek. But one day we find Christ again—and it is in such circumstances that the power of the Father's will becomes evident to us."[10]

In moments of spiritual aridity, we may feel like Mary and Joseph. We may feel that we have lost Christ. Our prayer seems dry and pointless. Our pious practices seem like chores. We search for him everywhere through all our familiar methods of prayer and devotion, but he is nowhere to be found. We do not understand.

Eventually, however, we find him again. And then we discover that Jesus has been with us all along. By withdrawing the pleasant consolations that initially attracted us to the spiritual life, Jesus invites us to come to him for *who* he is—not for the good feelings he may give us in prayer. In doing so, he calls us to a deeper level of trust and an even more intimate communion with him. While he may seem lost to us, he really is doing his "Father's business" in the interior temple of our souls.

FOUR

Scriptural Reflections on the Luminous Mysteries

In the Luminous Mysteries we encounter Jesus as the "light of the world" who overcomes the darkness. This light of Christ appears in the places we would least expect, shining into the dark corners of our existence.

Take, for example, the first mystery of light, Christ's baptism in the Jordan. Jesus, the sinless one, surprisingly enters the same waters of repentance that all the sinners have entered. And yet it is precisely in meeting the people in their act of repentance that Christ's divine light is manifested: The heavens open, and the Spirit descends upon him, while the Father's voice declares, "This is my beloved Son, with whom I am well pleased" (Mt 3:17).

In the second mystery, the wedding at Cana, the light of Christ is revealed in the water from the Jewish purification jars, which are used at the feast for ritual hand washing or utensil cleaning. Performing his first miracle, Jesus transforms the water from these jars into an abundance of good wine. This act may symbolize what Christ wants to do in all our hearts. He wants his light to fall on the dirty jars in our lives—our weaknesses, fears, and sins—so that they may be transformed with new life by his grace.

In the third mystery, the proclamation of the kingdom, John Paul II suggests that we focus on Christ's call to conversion and his forgiveness for those who humbly approach him. Once again, in this mystery we see Christ's light shining in the least expected places: on sinners, tax collectors, lepers, prostitutes, pagans, and all the other social and religious outcasts of the day who hear his call to repent and receive his forgiveness.

In the fourth luminous mystery, the Transfiguration, Christ's light is manifested at a most unusual time. Just after Jesus tells the apostles the startling news that he must go to Jerusalem to suffer and be crucified, he goes up a mountain with Peter, James, and John and allows them to witness his divine glory. By displaying his glory just after predicting his passion, the Transfiguration scene foreshadows how the glory of the Savior is revealed most fully not in worldly triumph, but in his sacrificial love on the cross.

Similarly, the final mystery, the institution of the Eucharist, is placed in the context of Christ's suffering. During the Last Supper his enemies are plotting his arrest, and one of his own apostles leaves the table to go betray him. Yet, here as the drama of his passion and death is about to unfold, Jesus leaves us the profound gift of himself in the Eucharist. Under the appearances of bread and wine the real presence of Christ's Body and Blood is made present to us today in the Mass. In this Holy Communion the divine light of Christ shines most intimately in the caverns of our souls, drawing us into deeper unity with our Lord.

The First Luminous Mystery:
Christ's Baptism in the Jordan
Matthew 3:13-17; Mark 1:9-11; Luke 3:21-22

John the baptizer appeared in the wilderness, preaching a baptism of repentance for the forgiveness of sins. And there went out to him all the country of Judea, and all the people of Jerusalem; and they were baptized by him in the river Jordan, confessing their sins.

MARK 1:4-5

The desert wilderness around the Jordan River does not seem to be the ideal place to start a movement. To get there from Jerusalem, one would have to travel several hours through rugged terrain and desert heat. Upon arrival, one would find himself at the lowest point on the face of the earth—some twelve hundred feet below sea level. From a modern perspective, one might say the Jordan River basin lies "in the middle of nowhere."

Nevertheless, multitudes of people from all over Jerusalem and the region of Judea gather to be a part of the movement John is starting there (see Mk 1:5). Religious groups such as the Sadducees and Pharisees, as well as tax collectors, soldiers, and prostitutes, all come out to participate in John's ritual of baptism and express their repentance (see Mt 3:7; 21:32; Lk 3:10-14). Why would they be so excited about going out to the Jordan wilderness?

No Ordinary River
For the Jews the Jordan River was not any ordinary water source. It was a river that symbolized new beginnings. Elijah the prophet was taken

up to heaven at the Jordan. Elisha, his successor, began his prophetic ministry at this same spot. Naaman the Syrian was cured of his leprosy at this river.

However, what made the Jordan stand out most for the Jews was its association with the Exodus story. After fleeing from slavery in Egypt and wandering in the desert for forty years, the Israelites finally entered the Promised Land by passing through the Jordan River. Thus the crossing of the Jordan represents the climax of the entire Exodus.

Jews in the first century were hoping for a new type of exodus in their lives. In fact, the prophets used the Exodus story as an image for what God would do in the messianic age. They foretold that one day God would free the people from their enemies, just as he once liberated their ancestors from Pharaoh in Egypt. Jews in John's day longed for these prophecies to be fulfilled. They believed God eventually would send Israel a new king, a Messiah, who would rescue them from their present-day oppressors and bring about the new exodus.

This helps explain why John chose to baptize in the Jordan. Although he could have baptized in many other locations, he chose the Jordan River because he wanted to send a powerful message: The new exodus is here. In inviting people to travel out into the desert, go down into the waters of the Jordan, and reenter the land, John was having the people reenact the Exodus story. Such a symbolic action expressed hope that the final great exodus was about to take place. It is no wonder there was so much enthusiasm and expectation surrounding John's movement!

The Baptism of the Sinless One

Then one day the Messiah finally arrives. Joining the large crowd of repentant sinners, Jesus comes to the Jordan to be baptized by John. Understandably, John does not feel worthy to baptize the Messiah. He humbly acknowledges his subordinate role of preparing the way for Jesus: "I need to be baptized by you, and do you come to me?" (Mt 3:14). Nevertheless, Jesus insists: "Let it be so now; for thus it is fitting for us to fulfil all righteousness" (Mt 3:15).

One can appreciate John's trepidation. After all, who would be worthy to baptize the Son of God? And still there is an even more puzzling question: *Why* would Jesus need to be baptized in the first place? If John's baptism symbolizes repentance of sins and Christians believe Jesus is sinless, why does he undergo this ritual of baptism?

Certainly Jesus does not *need* baptism or repentance, but he participates in this ritual in order to demonstrate his solidarity with Israel and all humanity. By going into the same waters that the repentant people have been entering, he shows us that he has come to unite himself to sinners so that they may be restored in him to the Father. In this action at the beginning of his messianic mission, Jesus foreshadows how he will bear the sins of all the world on the cross at the culmination of his public ministry. The *Cathechism* makes this point when explaining Christ's baptism: "He allows himself to be numbered among sinners; he is already 'the Lamb of God, who takes away the sins of the world.' Already he is anticipating the 'baptism' of his bloody death" (*CCC*, 536).

The Heavens Open

At the moment of his baptism, Jesus steps into the water and prays. Then, as he comes out of the water, "immediately he saw the heavens opened and the Spirit descending upon him like a dove; and a voice came from heaven, 'Thou art my beloved Son; with thee I am well pleased'" (Mk 1:10-11).

"The Spirit descending like a dove" recalls how God's Spirit hovered over the waters at the start of creation (see Gn 1:2). It also brings to mind how Noah sent out a dove that hovered over the waters of the renewed creation after the flood (see Gn 8:10-12). Now that same Spirit falls on Jesus in the waters of the Jordan and thus signals another new beginning for the world: The broken, divided human family is about to be recreated in the one family of God through Christ's Holy Spirit.

This biblical theme of God's Spirit coming upon the waters to renew all creation helps us to understand what really happens in the sacrament of baptism today. For in the waters of baptism we encounter that same Holy Spirit, and he once again comes to bring new life. At the moment of baptism God's Spirit fills our souls and transforms us with his supernatural life. We truly become new creations (see 2 Cor 5:17; Gal 6:15), adopted sons and daughters of God (see Gal 3:15–4:7). As a result of Christ's Spirit dwelling in our hearts, the heavenly Father now can say to us what he first said to Jesus at the Jordan, "You are my beloved Son."

The Lord's Servant

Finally, while the voice from heaven exalts Christ as the beloved Son in whom the Father is well pleased, it also foreshadows the painful road the Son must travel. Let us consider how these words from heaven recall a prophecy in the Old Testament about the servant of the Lord.

God foretold through Isaiah that he would send a faithful servant to fulfill his plan of salvation. God would rejoice in this servant, saying: "*Behold, my servant,* whom I uphold, my chosen, *in whom my soul delights;* I have put *my Spirit upon him*" (Is 42:1). This servant of the Lord would reunite all of Israel (see Is 49:5) and be a light to all the nations (see Is 42:6; 49:6). Yet this servant would accomplish God's redemptive plan through much suffering for our sins (see Is 53).

At Christ's baptism the Spirit descends on Jesus and the voice from heaven says: "Thou art my beloved Son; with thee I am well pleased."

These words echo Isaiah's prophecy about the servant of the Lord—the servant in whom the Father delights and on whom the Spirit rests. Jesus is thus presented as God's faithful servant who would be light to all the world. This servant, however, was expected to endure great suffering on account of our sins. Therefore, while this opening scene of Christ's public life exalts him as the Son of God anointed by the Holy Spirit, it also subtly foreshadows how Jesus will endure great affliction for our sins as the suffering servant from Isaiah. Indeed, Christ's messianic mission will culminate in his sacrifice on the cross.

The Second Luminous Mystery:
The Wedding Feast at Cana
John 2:1-11

On the third day there was a marriage at Cana in Galilee, and the mother of Jesus was there; Jesus also was invited to the marriage, with his disciples. When the wine failed, the mother of Jesus said to him, "They have no wine."

JOHN 2:1-3

Imagine the pain and embarrassment the newlyweds must feel over having run out of wine at their own wedding feast. Noticing the crisis at hand and moved with pity for them, Mary rushes to bring the problem to Jesus' attention. St. Thomas Aquinas says we should note Mary's kindness and mercy in this scene: "For it is a quality of mercy to regard another's distress as one's own, because to be merciful is to have a heart distressed at the distress of another."[1]

Furthermore, John Paul II sees in this act of kindness a pattern for

Mary's continued concern over the needs of all Christians. Just as Mary interceded on behalf of the couple at Cana, so she continues to bring our needs before her son. Thus this scene serves as an example of *"Mary's solicitude for human beings,* her coming to them in the wide variety of their wants and needs" and "bringing those needs within the radius of Christ's messianic mission."[2]

Most significantly, we also see that Mary has tremendous faith in her son. Jesus is just a guest; he does not have any wine at his disposal. Up to this point he has not performed any miracles. Therefore, from a natural perspective, Mary has no reason to ask him to help.

Still, when Mary notices that the wine has run out, her first instinct is to turn to Jesus. According to some commentators, such an unusual request only makes sense if she is expecting Jesus to work some extraordinary sign. Though she has yet to see her son work a single miracle, she has faith in his supernatural power and believes that he can help.

"Woman"

"And Jesus said to her, 'O woman, what have you to do with me? My hour has not yet come'" (Jn 2:4).

At first glance, Jesus seems a little harsh. His response to Mary's request appears to be disrespectful, perhaps even a rebuke, as if he were pushing his mother away. After all, how many children would dare to call their own mother *woman?*

However, as we continue reading the story, we see that Jesus is not in any way rejecting his mother or her request. Whatever the address *woman* may mean, Mary does not seem to interpret it negatively. Her response, in fact, suggests that she believes he will solve the problem promptly. She tells the servants, "Do whatever he tells you" (Jn 2:5).

Moreover, Jesus does not in any way reject Mary's request but responds to it favorably by changing the water to wine. So whatever this puzzling title *woman* may mean, it cannot be something harsh and negative.

When this passage is considered within the wider context of John's Gospel, the title *woman* takes on greater meaning. The Gospel of John begins the story of Jesus against the backdrop of the story of creation. The opening line of the Gospel is "*In the beginning* was the Word" (Jn 1:1)—a phrase taken right from the start of the creation story in Genesis 1:1, "In the beginning God created the heavens and the earth." John's Gospel then goes on to speak of creation, life, light, and light shining in the darkness—all images from the creation story (see Jn 1:1-5). By using this Genesis imagery, John is announcing that the arrival of Jesus marks a new beginning for the world. The coming of Christ will bring about a renewal of creation, which has been disrupted by sin.

Some commentators also point out that John's Gospel begins with a series of seven days, which establish a new creation week. In the first chapter John sets up a succession of four days, starting with John 1:1, "In the beginning." John 1:29 says "the next day," marking day number two. John 1:35 and 1:43 also say "the next day," accounting for days three and four. Then the second chapter begins by saying: "*On the third day* there was a marriage at Cana in Galilee" (Jn 2:1). The third day after the fourth day would represent the seventh day in John's Gospel. Thus the wedding feast at Cana takes place at the culmination of the "new creation week" in the Gospel of John, the seventh day.

A New Eve

Now we are prepared to understand more about the meaning of Jesus' response to Mary in this scene. At the climax of this new creation week, Jesus calls his mother "woman." Understood within the context of the Genesis background, the title "woman" would recall the woman of Genesis, Eve (see Gn 2:23). In this sense Mary can be seen as a new Eve—a perspective that Christians from as early as the second century have held. Whereas the first Eve cooperated in the fall of humanity, Mary, the new Eve, cooperates in the redemption of the human family.

As St. Irenaeus once said, "[T]he knot of Eve's disobedience was untied through the obedience of Mary. For what the virgin Eve had tied through unbelief, the Virgin set free through faith."[3]

As the faithful new Eve, Mary tells the servants, "Do whatever he tells you" (Jn 2:5). Here we see Mary serving as a spokeswoman for her son's will, exhorting others to trust in Jesus' commands. Indeed, following Jesus' instructions requires a lot of trust on the servants' part because he asks them to do something very strange with the six stone jars for the Jewish rites of purification that are standing there. These jars probably would have been used at the feast for ritual hand washing or cleansing of utensils (see Mk 7:3-4). What is astounding is that Jesus commands the servants to fill these jars with water and bring some of their contents to the steward of the feast.

However odd such a request might seem, the servants obediently carry out Jesus' desire—despite their own uncertainty about how this will resolve the problem. Imagine their trepidation as they watch their boss taste the water. And imagine their great surprise when they witness his joyful response. Not knowing where it came from, the steward calls the bridegroom and says to him, "Every man serves the good wine first; and when men have drunk freely, then the poor wine; but you have kept the good wine until now" (Jn 2:10).

In this first of Christ's miracles, the servants discover the amazing things that happen when people trust Jesus. John Paul II commented on how Mary's command, "Do whatever he tells you," continues to have meaning for our lives today: "It is an exhortation to trust without hesitation, especially when one does not understand the meaning or benefit of what Christ asks."[4] Thus we are called to have faith like the servants, trusting Christ's will for our lives and doing whatever he tells us, even when the pathway may be unclear or the outcome uncertain.

The Good Wine

"This, the first of his signs, Jesus did at Cana in Galilee, and manifested his glory; and his disciples believed in him" (Jn 2:11).

This first of Jesus' miracles sets the tone for understanding his entire public ministry. The water being transformed into "good wine" can symbolize the movement from the Old Covenant to the New. On one hand, water from the Jewish rites of purification would serve as a symbol of the old covenant, which is reaching its culmination in Christ. On the other hand, the prophets used the image of overflowing wine to symbolize the blessings God would bestow on Israel in the messianic age (see Is 25:6; Jer 31:12; Jl 3:18; Am 9:13). Therefore, Jesus' miracle of turning the water from the ritual cleansing jars into an overabundance of wine expresses the fact that the new covenant era is here. Furthermore, what Christ has done in those dirty purification jars he wishes to do in each of us: *cleanse us* of our sins and *transform us* into "good wine."

The Third Luminous Mystery:
The Proclamation of the Kingdom
Mark 1:14; Matthew 6:25-27; Luke 15:11-24

This third mystery of light offers much to contemplate, for it encompasses practically the entirety of Christ's public ministry. Yet, in his apostolic letter on the rosary, John Paul II suggests two themes in particular for us to ponder when praying this mystery: Christ's *call to conversion* and his *forgiving the sins* of those who come to him in humble trust.

While numerous scenes from Christ's proclamation of the kingdom could be considered, this reflection will focus on just a few passages that exemplify the themes the pope has recommended. Let us begin by considering the call to conversion.

The Call to Conversion

"Jesus came into Galilee, preaching the gospel of God, and saying, 'The time is fulfilled, and the kingdom of God is at hand; repent, and believe in the gospel'" (Mk 1:14-15).

One basic meaning of *conversion* is "to turn." Throughout the Bible, when God calls his people to repentance, he is inviting them to reorient their lives—to turn away from sin and *turn back* to him. This involves an honest evaluation of one's life. We must ask, "What is truly at the center of my life? Do I live as if God is at the very center of all I desire, all I strive for, all I do? Or is there something else—such as wealth, status, achievement, approval, or pleasure—that I am hoping will bring me fulfillment, security, and happiness?"

One passage from Christ's proclamation of the kingdom that challenges us to make such a self-assessment and to realign our lives accordingly comes from the Sermon on the Mount:

"Therefore I tell you, do not be anxious about your life, what you shall eat or what you shall drink, nor about your body, what you shall put on. Is not life more than food, and the body more than clothing? Look at the birds of the air: they neither sow nor reap nor gather into barns, and yet your heavenly Father feeds them. Are you not of more value than they? And which of you by being anxious can add one cubit to his span of life?...

"Therefore do not be anxious, saying, 'What shall we eat?' or 'What shall we drink?' or 'What shall we wear?' For the Gentiles seek all these things; and your heavenly Father knows that you need them all. But seek first his kingdom and his righteousness, and all these things shall be yours as well" (Mt 6:25-33).

One helpful way to discern what we put at the center of our lives is to consider what we worry about. That is what Jesus challenges us to ponder in these verses. It is as if he were telling us, "Do not be anxious saying, 'What shall we eat, What shall we drink? How will we make the car payment? What does she think of me? How will I get everything done this week? Did I leave a good impression?'" When something causes us great anxiety or worry, it is often a sign that we are not seeking *first* Christ's kingdom. We have allowed something other than God to move into the center of our lives. We are in need of a realignment.

Seeking First the Kingdom

It is important to note that Jesus does not say that these worldly concerns are bad. God certainly wants us to pay the bills, strive for excellence in our work, find good friendships, and have food on the table. "Your heavenly Father knows that you need them all," Jesus says. It is just that these things cannot sustain us at the center of our being, for they cannot make us truly happy. When we treat finite pleasures, successes, possessions, or honors like an infinite god, a source of lasting fulfillment and security, they will fall short every time. When they creep into the center, they will leave us feeling empty, frustrated ... and very anxious about our lives.

That is why Jesus goes on to say, "But seek first his kingdom and his righteousness, and all these things shall be yours as well." If God's will is truly our first priority, the other areas of our lives tend to fall into place because they are centered on the one sure foundation. When we put our trust in the One who knows our needs far better than we do, all our desires and longings tend to find a certain harmony, since they are centered around Christ. Thus the call to conversion involves an ongoing turning back to God, as we entrust more of our lives to him and desire to live with him at the center of our hearts.

Forgiveness of Sins

In this mystery of the rosary, John Paul II also suggests that we contemplate Christ's forgiving the sins of those who come to him in humble trust. This second theme flows from the first, the call to conversion. While discerning what keeps us from living with Christ at the center of our lives, it can be a difficult moment when we discover the hard truth about ourselves—the truth about how proud, self-centered, envious, cowardly, lustful, or critical we really are. Yet it is precisely in this humbling realization of our own tragic flaws and weaknesses that God meets us with his mercy and gives the sinner hope.

St. Bernard of Clairvaux once said that the stark reality of this painful truth about ourselves would be intolerable without the grace of God's mercy. That is why Bernard would not allow himself to focus exclusively on the fact of his own sinfulness but would look at his broken condition in the light of God's mercy: "As for me, as long as I look at myself, my eye is filled with bitterness. But if I look up and fix my eyes on the aid of the divine mercy, this happy vision of God soon tempers the bitter vision of myself."[5]

This is how the woman caught in adultery must have felt. The scribes and Pharisees throw this woman in front of Jesus to use her as a test case to trap him. They ask Jesus if she should be stoned, since the Law of Moses prescribes such a penalty for women who commit adultery (see Jn 8:2-11).

Roman law, however, prohibits the Jews from issuing capital punishment on their own. If Jesus agrees to stone her, he will be in trouble with the Romans. If he tells them not to stone her, they will accuse him of being unfaithful to the Law of Moses. Jesus is being set up, and there does not seem to be any way to answer their question without facing much hostility.

A Ministry of Mercy

Jesus, however, not only avoids the trap but takes the conversation to a completely new level. The scribes and Pharisees focus on a legal issue, while Jesus focuses on the person. Jesus challenges them to consider the way of forgiveness instead of the path of condemnation:

"And as they continued to ask him, he stood up and said to them, 'Let him who is without sin among you be the first to throw a stone at her.' ... But when they heard it, they went away, one by one, beginning with the eldest, and Jesus was left alone with the woman standing before him. Jesus looked up and said to her, 'Woman, where are they? Has no one condemned you?' She said, 'No one, Lord.' And Jesus said, 'Neither do I condemn you; go, and do not sin again'" (Jn 8:7, 9-11).

Accused, shamed, and now used as a pawn in the Pharisees' dispute with Jesus, the woman stands humiliated before the crowd. At this moment Jesus lifts the burden of her sin: "Let him who is without sin among you be the first to throw a stone at her." None of the scribes and Pharisees condemn her, and neither does Jesus. While he does not overlook her adultery (he tells her, "Do not sin again"), neither does he come as a judge simply to evaluate the legal fact of her sin. Yes, she has broken the moral law, and yes, she has sinned. But Jesus focuses on the person, not just the legal facts, and he comes to offer her his mercy. He gives her the chance to "turn back" to God and sin no more.

This is the splendor of Christ's ministry of mercy. He comes to us sinners not as a harsh prosecuting attorney, suspecting the worst in our actions, doubting our motives, and ready to condemn. Rather, he comes as our Savior, offering us understanding, forgiveness, and the opportunity to start over again—as long as we "turn back" to him at the center of our lives.

It is no wonder that John Paul II mentions the sacrament of reconciliation when discussing this third luminous mystery, for it is in this sacrament that the kingdom's call to conversion and ministry of mercy are most fully realized.[6] In humbly recognizing the truth of our failings before God, we begin the process of conversion. When we confess our sins in the sacrament of reconciliation, we can experience the Father's forgiveness, as well as Jesus' powerful grace to help us turn and live with him again at the center of our lives.

The Fourth Luminous Mystery:
The Transfiguration
Matthew 17:1-8

The Transfiguration represents a unique moment in the life of Jesus. Throughout his public ministry, the fullness of Christ's glory has been veiled. Now, however, Peter, James, and John catch a glimpse of that glory as they witness his face shining like the sun and his garments becoming a dazzling white.

They see Jesus speaking with two leading men from Israelite history who together represent the entire old covenant: Moses, who symbolizes the Law, and Elijah, who symbolizes the prophets. Amidst this conversation, a bright cloud filled with God's glory suddenly overshadows them, and the apostles hear a heavenly voice saying, "This is my beloved Son with whom I am well pleased; listen to him" (Mt 17:5).

What is the purpose behind this spectacular display of Jesus' glory? Why is Jesus transfigured at this point in his public ministry? The context surrounding this scene helps us to appreciate the significance of this turning point in Christ's life.

The Road to Jerusalem

In the scene just before the Transfiguration, Jesus confirmed for the apostles what they all had been suspecting and hoping. He told them that he was indeed Israel's Messiah (see Mt 16:16-20).

Jesus, however, immediately made it clear that his mission as the Messiah-King would not take him to a luxurious royal palace or a triumphant military victory. Rather, his messianic mission would lead him to the cross: "From that time Jesus began to show his disciples that he must go to Jerusalem and suffer many things from the elders and chief priests and scribes, and be killed, and on the third day be raised" (Mt 16:21).

Understandably, this message did not go over well with the apostles. How could Israel's Messiah-King suffer such a horrible death? Even Peter was in shock, saying: "God forbid, Lord! This shall never happen to you" (Mt 16:22).

Now, six days later, Jesus embarks on his final journey to Jerusalem. And his first step on the way is significant. He takes Peter, James, and John up a mountain to prepare them for the difficult road ahead. Jesus knows that when they arrive in Jerusalem, their faith will be tested like never before. They will see their master arrested, beaten, humiliated, stripped, and nailed to a cross. Before they face that trial of faith, Jesus gives them the opportunity to see him in his glory, so that when they see him in his utter humiliation, they might remember that he is the Messiah, the glorified Son of God.

The Byzantine Catholic liturgy expresses this point in a prayer for the Feast of the Transfiguration: "You were transfigured on the mountain, and your disciples, as much as they were capable of it, beheld your glory, O Christ our God, so that when they should see you crucified they would understand that your Passion was voluntary, and proclaim to the world that you truly are the splendor of the Father."[7]

A New Moses

"And after six days Jesus took with him Peter and James and John his brother, and led them up a high mountain apart. And he was transfigured before them, and his face shone like the sun.... And behold, there appeared to them Moses and Elijah, talking with him.... He was still speaking, when lo, a bright cloud overshadowed them, and a voice from the cloud said, 'This is my beloved Son, with whom I am well pleased; listen to him.' When the disciples heard this, they fell on their faces, and were filled with awe" (Mt 17:1-3, 5-6).

Accompanying Jesus up the mountain, Peter, James, and John see their master in a completely new light. And what they experience on this high mountain would remind them of what happened to Moses at another famous mountain, Mount Sinai, during another turning point in the history of salvation.

In a key moment from the Exodus story, the Israelite people set up camp at Mount Sinai to establish the old covenant, which sealed them as God's chosen people. While there, Moses led three of his closest associates—Aaron, Nadab, and Abihu—up the mountain, and the glory of the Lord covered them in the form of a cloud for six days. On the seventh day a voice called out from the cloud to give Moses the Ten Commandments on tablets of stone (see Ex 24:9-17).

During their stay at Sinai Moses' face was shining brightly because he had been talking with God in the sanctuary. When the people saw his radiant face, they were in awe and were afraid to come near him (see Ex 34:29-30).

In similar fashion, Jesus is about to establish the new covenant, and he too goes up a high mountain. Like Moses, Jesus brings with him three of his closest coworkers—Peter, James, and John. While atop the mountain, Christ's face shines brightly, and the three apostles fall down full of awe, reminiscent of the Israelites' reaction to Moses' radiant face. At the height of the Transfiguration scene, God's glory cloud comes down on the mountain and overshadows them, as it covered Moses and the Israelite leaders on Sinai. And just as a heavenly voice called out from the cloud to give Moses the old law on the tablets of stone, so now the Father's voice calls out from the cloud to reveal the new law in the person of Jesus: "This is my beloved Son, with whom I am well pleased; listen to him."

The Glorified Face of Christ

Despite the similarities between these two scenes, Matthew is careful to note how Jesus clearly outshines Moses. The new covenant is greater than the old. Moses' face was simply described as shining; Jesus' face is described as shining brightly "like the sun." And he is radiating the divine glory so much that even his garments appear as "white as light" (Mt 17:2).

Moreover, while this event may reveal the glory of Christ's divinity, it also manifests his glorified humanity. Having a shining face does not necessarily mean one is divine. Moses' shining face on Mount Sinai simply showed that he *reflected* the glory of God. Thus, when we contemplate the transfigured Jesus, we see not only a glimpse of his divinity but also a view of his glorified humanity, which perfectly reflects God's glory.

In turn, we also see a snapshot of how our own fallen humanity is meant to be healed, perfected, and clothed with the glory of God—a theme found in St. Paul's Second Letter to the Corinthians. Paul views the transfiguration of Moses' face (and in the background, the transfiguration of Christ's face) as a sign of the transformation God wants to bring about in all our lives: "And we all, with unveiled face, beholding the glory of the Lord, are being changed into his likeness from one degree of glory to another; for this comes from the Lord who is the

Spirit" (2 Cor 3:18). Indeed, through Christ's transforming grace we are called to live in a way that reflects the glory of God here on earth. Jesus calls us to be *changed into his likeness from one degree of glory to another.*

The Suffering Servant
"This is my beloved Son, with whom I am well pleased; listen to him"
(Mt 17:5).

Coming just six days after Jesus told the apostles about his upcoming death in Jerusalem, these words from the Father will help assure them that Jesus really is the Messiah and the Son of God. At the same time, these words show the stark reality of Christ's mission to suffer for our sins, for they bring to mind the suffering servant figure from the prophet Isaiah.

As we saw in our consideration of the similar words spoken by the Father at Christ's baptism, Isaiah foretold that God would send an anointed servant to restore Israel and bring salvation to all the nations. God would rejoice in this faithful one, saying, "Behold my servant, whom I uphold, my chosen, in whom my soul delights" (Is 42:1). This servant too would be "wounded for our transgressions" and "bruised for our iniquities" (Is 53:5). Like a lamb led to the slaughter, the Lord's servant would make himself "an offering for sin" (Is 52:7, 10).

Thus, while the Transfiguration exalts Christ and shows forth his glory, the scene again foreshadows Christ's destiny as the suffering servant who will die in Jerusalem for the sins of all humanity. Ultimately, these two themes of Christ's glory and his suffering are meant to go together, for God's glory will be revealed most fully not in worldly splendor or self-exaltation but in his self-giving love for us on the cross. And these themes of the Transfiguration stand as a reminder to us: We are called to radiate God's glory most splendidly through our own sacrificial love here on earth.

The Fifth Luminous Mystery:
The Institution of the Eucharist
Luke 22:14-23

I have earnestly desired to eat this passover with you before I suffer; for I tell you I shall not eat it until it is fulfilled in the kingdom of God.

LUKE 22:15-16

The annual Passover ritual was the principal festival for the Jews because it celebrated one of the most important moments in Israel's history: the first Passover in Egypt. On that night God instructed the enslaved Israelite people to sacrifice a lamb, eat it, and put its blood on their doorposts. It was their last supper in Egypt, for on that night, the Israelites escaped from bondage, and the angel of death struck down all the Egyptian firstborn sons. Every year thereafter the Jews retold and reenacted the Passover story in their homes and at the temple to celebrate God's great act of liberation in the Exodus.

Back to the Future

What is important for us to note is that the Jews celebrated the Passover feast as a *memorial.* For the ancient Jews, a liturgical memorial did much more than simply recall a past event. It made that past event present. As a memorial, this annual meal celebration was believed to make the first Passover in Egypt mystically present to those celebrating the ritual.

This is why Jews in Jesus' day believed that when they celebrated the Passover meal, the events surrounding that first Passover in Egypt were brought before them, so that they could be at one with their ancestors and participate in that foundational moment of their nation's history. In fact, some ancient Jews commented that when they celebrated the Passover meal each year, it was as if they themselves were walking out of Egypt with their ancestors in the Exodus.

Furthermore, the Passover not only made the past mystically present but also looked to the future. In Jesus' day the Passover feast was charged with messianic expectations. There was hope that on some Passover night in the future, God would send the Messiah to the city of Jerusalem to liberate the people. On that much anticipated night, God would rescue the Jews from their present-day oppressors, just as he freed them from the Egyptians on the night of the first Passover.

With this background in mind, imagine the apostles' great excitement when Jesus gathers them in Jerusalem to celebrate the Passover. Earlier that week Jesus entered the royal city of Jerusalem and was hailed as a king. Now he tells them it is time to celebrate the Passover. Given the messianic hopes being pinned on Jesus that week and the messianic expectations associated with the Passover each year, this clearly is not going to be any ordinary Passover celebration for the apostles. If Jesus is the Messiah and he has been received as a king in Jerusalem, his calling the apostles together for the freedom meal of the Passover can only signal one thing: The Passover of Passovers is finally here. The new exodus is about to begin in the Upper Room tonight. Christ's entire public ministry reaches its culmination in this Last Supper. No wonder he says, "I have earnestly desired to eat this passover with you" (Lk 22:15).

Where Is the Lamb?

What is most odd about the Gospel accounts of the Last Supper is that none of them mention the most important part of the Passover meal:

the lamb. Not only was the lamb the main course, but it also served as the primary reminder of how the Passover lambs were sacrificed in Egypt so that the Israelite firstborn sons would not be killed in the tenth plague. Yet the Gospel accounts of the Last Supper focus on another type of sacrifice taking place:

"And he took bread, and when he had given thanks he broke it and gave it to them, saying, 'This is my body which is given for you. Do this in remembrance of me.' And likewise the cup after supper, saying, 'This cup which is poured out for you is the new covenant in my blood'" (Lk 22:19-20).

Here Jesus speaks about a body being "given" and blood being "poured out." Every Jew there would recognize that this is sacrificial language taken from the rituals in the temple, where the bodies of the animals are "offered up" and their blood "poured out" over the altar. At this particular Passover meal, however, the body being offered is not that of a lamb or any other animal. Instead, Jesus speaks of *his own* body being sacrificed and *his own* blood being poured out. In other words, Jesus identifies himself with the Passover lamb. Just as the Passover lamb was sacrificed in Egypt to spare the firstborn sons of Israel, so now Jesus is about to be sacrificed on the cross to spare the lot of all humanity.

The Last Supper and the Cross

In this sense, Christ's sacrifice on the cross begins with his institution of the Eucharist at the Last Supper. There in the Upper Room Jesus voluntarily offers up his body and blood as the Passover Lamb. All that is left is for that sacrifice to be carried out externally in his body on Calvary.

Therefore, when Jesus institutes the Eucharist and says, "Do this in remembrance [as a memorial] of me," he is speaking of his sacrificial self-offering. In the Jewish sense of *memorial*, Jesus is commanding the apostles to *make present* the sacrifice of his body and blood, his total gift of love, which he offers at the Last Supper and carries out on Calvary. The Eucharist is the new Passover of the new covenant.

This is why Catholics speak of the Mass as a sacrifice. It is not a new sacrifice, but makes present the one sacrifice of Christ: "When the Church celebrates the Eucharist, she commemorates Christ's Passover, and it is made present: the sacrifice Christ offered once for all on the cross remains ever present" (*CCC*, 1364). As a biblical memorial, the Passover ritual enabled the Jews to participate in the founding event of their nationhood, the Exodus, which was made present to them in the annual celebration of this feast. Similarly, as the principal memorial of the new covenant, the Eucharist allows us to share in the founding event of Christianity, Jesus' offering of himself on the cross.

Consequently, the *Catechism* teaches that in the Mass, we offer in prayer our entire lives in union with Christ's offering to the Father: "In the Eucharist the sacrifice of Christ becomes also the sacrifice of the members of his Body. The lives of the faithful, their praise, sufferings, prayer, and work are united with those of Christ and with his total offering.... Christ's sacrifice present on the altar makes it possible for all generations of Christians to be united with his offering" (*CCC*, 1368).

The Real Presence

Finally, at the Last Supper, Jesus gives us his very body and blood in the Eucharist under the appearances of bread and wine. For the ancient Jews *the body* expressed the person's soul, and *the blood* was believed to contain the person's life. From this perspective, we can see that in the Eucharist, Jesus intends to give himself completely to us in this sacrament of love.

By giving us his body and blood, Christ forges the most profound union we can have with him here on earth. Indeed, reception of the Eucharist is called "Holy Communion" for it is communion with Jesus himself—his body, blood, soul, and divinity. As the true "Bread of Life," Jesus himself tells us that the Eucharist is vital for our union with him: "He who eats my flesh and drinks my blood has eternal life, and I will raise him up at the last day. For my flesh is food indeed, and my blood is drink indeed. He who eats my flesh and drinks my blood abides in me, and I in him. As the living Father sent me, and I live because of the Father, so he who eats me will live because of me" (Jn 6:54-57).

FIVE

Scriptural Reflections on the Sorrowful Mysteries

John Paul II says the Sorrowful Mysteries represent "the culmination of the revelation of God's love."[1] Beginning with the agony in the garden, Jesus confronts all the temptations and sins of humanity and says to the Father, "Not as I will, but as thou wilt" (Mt 26:39). Indeed, Christ's "yes" in the Garden of Gethsemane reverses the "no" of Adam in the Garden of Eden.

Yet Christ's love and fidelity come at a price. Jesus firmly resolves to do the Father's will in the first sorrowful mystery, but this will lead him to the scourging at the pillar, the crowning with thorns, the carrying of the cross, and the crucifixion.[2] This is why, when discussing the Sorrowful Mysteries, John Paul II gives most of his attention to the agony in the garden. He says the other four Sorrowful Mysteries are the result of the first, and they highlight how Christ's loving commitment to the Father's will entails great suffering and sacrifice for the sake of our salvation.[3]

In addition to showing God's love for us, these Sorrowful Mysteries unveil the meaning of man himself. The pope says that Christ's self-giving love in his passion and death serves as the model for understanding the vocation of *all* human beings. We will only find fulfillment by making ourselves a sincere gift to others, as Jesus did for us on Calvary. Indeed, true love and faithfulness ultimately lead to the cross.

The First Sorrowful Mystery:
The Agony in the Garden
Matthew 26:36-46; Luke 22:39-46

The devil's assault against Jesus reaches a new peak here in the Garden of Gethsemane. This is not the first time these two have dueled. Before the start of Christ's public ministry the devil put Jesus to the test three times in the desert. Jesus resisted each of the devil's temptations, and the angels came to minister to him.

While Jesus could claim an initial victory in that battle in the desert, the war was far from over. As Luke's Gospel ominously notes, "When the devil had ended every temptation, he departed from him *until an opportune time*" (Lk 4:13). In other words, the devil was waiting for the right time to come back and put Jesus to the test again.

That "opportune time" of the devil has arrived in the Garden of Gethsemane in this first sorrowful mystery. Although Jesus engaged in several skirmishes with demons throughout his proclamation of the kingdom, he has not had to face a frontal assault from the devil until this night. In the events surrounding this scene, Luke's Gospel high-lights how Satan is mounting his final attack: The devil has just entered Judas (see Lk 22:3-4), Satan seeks to have all the disciples be sifted like wheat (see Lk 22:31), and Jesus describes his arrest as "the power of darkness" coming upon him (Lk 22:53). Luke makes this point clear: The final battle is about to begin.

Lead Us Not Into Temptation

As Jesus enters the garden with his disciples, he tells them, "Pray that you may not enter into temptation" (Lk 22:40). The word in New

Testament Greek for *temptation* is *peirasmos*, which is the same word used to describe the temptations that Satan inflicted on Christ in the desert. With this exhortation in the garden, Jesus signals that the hour of the devil's most severe testing is here. Just as he himself did not give in to the devil's testing in the desert, Jesus encourages the disciples to resist the testing that they are about to face as they witness their master being arrested, condemned, scourged, and crucified.

These words of Jesus also echo the last lines of the Lord's Prayer, which he taught the disciples earlier in his public ministry: "And lead us not into temptation (*peirasmos*)" (Mt 6:13; see Lk 11:4). While God may allow people to be tested in order to strengthen their faith, Jesus asks his disciples both in the Lord's Prayer and here again in Gethsemane to pray that they not "enter into" those tests in the sense of giving in to them. In other words, they are to pray that they may not yield to the trials that they are about to endure (see *CCC*, 2846).

Sorrowful Unto Death

Jesus then invites three of his apostles—Peter, James, and John—to come with him as he begins to pray on his own (see Mt 26:37). These are the same three who witnessed Christ's face shining brightly with God's glory at the Transfiguration. Now they will be near Jesus as the sweat from his face becomes like drops of blood in this moment of greatest agony (see Lk 22:44).

Troubled and afflicted, Jesus says to these three close friends, "My soul is very sorrowful, even to death; remain here, and watch with me" (Mt 26:38). To be sorrowful unto death means to be pushed to the extreme limits with grief. It describes almost unendurable suffering. Spoken in the context of Judas' betrayal and Christ's imminent arrest, Jesus' sorrow echoes the words of Sirach 37:2: "Is it not a grief to the death when a companion and friend turns to enmity?"

Knowing all that is about to happen to him, Jesus kneels down and falls on his face—highlighting his distress and the intensity of the prayer that follows: "Father, if it be possible, let this cup pass from me; nevertheless, not as I will, but as thou wilt" (Mt 26:39; see Lk 22:42).

At first glance this is a perplexing prayer. What does it mean? Is Jesus, at the last moment, trying to back out of his mission to redeem the world? Is he trying to persuade the Father to find another option, so he can avoid drinking "the cup" of suffering on Calvary?

Pass the Cup?

"If possible, let this cup pass from me." This prayer simply reflects the fact that Jesus is truly a man. Suffering and death are repulsive to human nature. If Jesus is truly human, the suffering that he is about to endure on the cross would not be perceived as something pleasant. As the *Catechism* explains, Christ's prayer in Gethsemane "expresses the horror that death represented for his human nature" (*CCC*, 612).

At the same time, unlike our weak wills wounded by sin, Jesus' human will is perfectly united to the Father's (see *CCC*, 475). Thus he immediately says, "Not as I will, but as thou wilt." In other words, while Christ feels a full aversion to death in his human nature, he also is completely willing to embrace that suffering on the cross for the sake of carrying out his Father's plan of salvation.

In the face of suffering we, in our fallen humanity, often hesitate to do the right thing, or we even shrink altogether from doing God's will. Too often we are afraid to make sacrifices, and we let our fear of suffering keep us from doing what is right. Jesus, however, faces that suffering, feels the full force of it, and freely embraces it for the sake of our salvation, in full acceptance of his Father's will.

The Agony

"And there appeared to him an angel from heaven, strengthening him. And being in an agony he prayed more earnestly; and his sweat became like great drops of blood falling down upon the ground" (Lk 22:43-44).

In response to Jesus' prayer, the Father sends an angel to strengthen him for his passion and death. Just as the angels ministered to him during his first battle with Satan in the desert (see Mt 4:11), so now an angel of the Lord comes to his aid as the devil's final onslaught is about to begin. The description of Jesus' sweat becoming like drops of blood shows the intensity of his ordeal. The turmoil in Jesus' soul is manifested through his body.

Some scholars have suggested that Luke's description of Jesus being in "agony" recalls the ordeal ancient runners faced as they were about to begin a race. As they approached the starting line, the runners sometimes would become so intense that sweat would break out all over their bodies. This moment was known as the runner's "agony."[4]

In the Garden of Gethsemane, Jesus faces an agony of his own as he begins a much more serious contest, a battle with the devil for the salvation of the world. Poised at the starting line of this redemptive contest, Jesus, like a runner, sweats profusely, manifesting the intensity of the ordeal he is about to undergo.

Back to Paradise

Finally, in this scene we can see Jesus reliving the test of Adam and proving himself to be a faithful Son of God precisely where Adam was unfaithful. For example, Adam was tested by the devil in the Garden of Eden, and Jesus is tested in the Garden of Gethsemane. Adam did not trust the Father in his time of testing, preferring his own will to God's; whereas Jesus says to the Father, "Not as I will, but as thou wilt." Adam's disobedience led him to the forbidden Tree of Knowledge of Good and

Evil, while Christ's prayer of obedience leads him to the wood of the cross—which Christians later will call the new Tree of Life.

As the new Adam, Jesus takes on the effects of Adam's sin. Consider how as a result of the first sin, Adam became ashamed in his *nakedness*, was *expelled from Paradise*, and received a number of curses. God said to Adam, "Cursed is the ground because of you; in toil you shall eat of it all the days of your life; thorns and thistles it shall bring forth to you;... In the sweat of your face you shall eat bread till you return to the ground, for out of it you were taken; you are dust, and to dust you shall return" (Gn 3:17-19). Adam's labor would no longer be easy. Now he had to toil in *sweat*, and the ground would often produce *thorns* and thistles instead of fruit. The greatest curse of all was *death*. Adam no longer would live forever but would return to the *ground* at the end of his life.

Taking on the curses of Adam, Jesus *sweats* intensely in Gethsemane as he clings to his Father's will. On Good Friday he is crowned with *thorns*, stripped *naked*, and nailed to a cross. His body returns to the *ground* as he is buried in a *garden* near Calvary (see Jn 19:41). Yet, while dying on the cross, Jesus announces that he is returning to Paradise and beginning to take the sons of Adam with him. One of the first to enter his kingdom is the "good thief," to whom Jesus says, "Today you will be with me in *Paradise*" (Lk 23:43).

As the new Adam, Jesus is faithful where the first Adam was unfaithful and takes on the curses which have plagued the human family since the Fall. In his passion and death, Christ thus undoes the first sin and restores the sons of Adam to the Father.

The Second Sorrowful Mystery:

The Scourging at the Pillar
Matthew 27:15-26

In matters of legal discipline, the Jews showed at least some restraint in their use of the whip. In order to ensure that whippings would not get out of hand, a criminal could be given up to forty lashes, depending on the offense committed (see Dt 25:3). Furthermore, the Pharisees, who worried that some enthusiastic executioners might accidentally cross over that legal limit, set the maximum amount of lashes at thirty-nine.

Roman scourging was not nearly as merciful. The practice itself was much more severe than a whipping, and there were no limits. A Roman scourging normally involved the prisoner's being stripped and tied to a pillar or a low post. The whip had leather thongs with sharp pieces of bone or metal spikes that would rip a person's flesh in a single stroke. If used repeatedly on a criminal's back, wounds would be torn open further, cutting into the muscle and exposing the person's bones. Scourgings sometimes even caused death.

A Roman scourging was not simply another form of punishment. Sometimes it was used to torture prisoners in order to extract information from them. Other times it served as a prelude to crucifixion, intended to inflict intense physical trauma before the prisoner carried his cross. In this latter case, scourging not only increased the suffering of the prisoner but also allowed the Roman soldiers some control over how long the prisoner would survive. A long, severe beating would greatly weaken the prisoner and result in a quicker death on the cross.

This latter type of scourging is what Jesus went through on Good Friday. It was his first step toward the cross, by which he would redeem the world.

The Barabbas Choice

What led to Jesus' being scourged at the pillar in the first place?

After being arrested and put on trial, Jesus was condemned to death by the Jewish leaders in Jerusalem. However, since they are under Roman law, they cannot carry out capital punishment on their own. Only the Roman government has the authority to execute. That is why the chief priests hand Jesus over to Pontius Pilate, the Roman governor ruling Judea. They charge that Jesus is a revolutionary who stirs up the people, and they want Pilate to have him executed (see Lk 23:2, 5).

Pilate, however, is used to dealing with rebels, and he realizes that Jesus is no serious threat to the Roman Empire. Pilate understands that what really lies at the heart of the chief priests' contention against this innocent man is a religious rivalry: "He knew it was out of envy that they had delivered him up" (Mt 27:18).

Since Pilate has a custom of freeing one Jewish prisoner during Passover, he offers to release Jesus. However, the chief priests and the crowds they incite ask for the release of another man named Barabbas, a notorious insurrectionist.

This is not simply a choice between a revolutionary criminal and an innocent man. There is much symbolism in this choice, for the name Barabbas literally means "son of the father." In choosing Barabbas, the crowds favor this false "son of the father," who as a Jewish rebel represents violence and vengeance. In the process they reject Jesus, the true Son of the Father, who represents peace and forgiveness.

"Pilate said to them, 'Then what shall I do with Jesus who is called Christ?' They all said, 'Let him be crucified.' And he said, 'Why, what evil has he done?' But they shouted all the more, 'Let him be crucified'" (Mt 27:22-23).

Pilate's Conscience

"So when Pilate saw that he was gaining nothing, but rather that a riot was beginning, he took water and washed his hands before the crowd, saying, 'I am innocent of this righteous man's blood; see to it yourselves.' And all the people answered, 'His blood be on us and on our children!' Then he released for them Barabbas, and having scourged Jesus, delivered him to be crucified" (Mt 27:24-26).

The opposition is too strong. Pilate realizes that he cannot convince the crowd and that their hostility is mounting to a riot. Rather than take a stand to protect the innocent Jesus, Pilate cowardly caves in to the pressure and allows Jesus to be scourged and crucified. In an effort to quell his troubled conscience, Pilate washes his hands in a symbolic gesture, intending to distance himself from responsibility for Christ's death.

History, however, will not let Pilate get away with that, for he will be immortalized in the Creed as the Roman ruler who allowed Jesus to be killed. To this very day, Christians all over the world continue to recall the tragic result of Pilate's lack of courage: "He suffered under Pontius Pilate, was crucified, died, and was buried."

The Third Sorrowful Mystery:
The Crowning With Thorns
Matthew 27:27-29

Imagine hundreds of Roman soldiers kneeling before a man who is crowned, clothed in a royal cloak, and holding a scepter in his right hand. They all fall down before him and give him homage, saying, "Hail, the King!"

In most contexts such a display would demonstrate a king's royal splendor. In the third sorrowful mystery, however, this scene represents the height of humiliation as the Roman soldiers scoff at Jesus and ridicule his claim to be the king of the Jews.

Hail to the King

"Then the soldiers of the governor took Jesus into the praetorium, and they gathered the whole battalion before him. And they stripped him and put a scarlet robe upon him, and plaiting a crown of thorns they put it on his head, and put a reed in his right hand. And kneeling before him they mocked him, saying, 'Hail, King of the Jews!'" (Mt 27:27-29).

The praetorium was the official residence of Pilate, the Roman governor. After being scourged, Jesus is taken there as one final stop on the way to his crucifixion. Matthew notes that "a whole battalion," which is a cohort of up to six hundred soldiers, meets him there to make sport of his claim to be Israel's Messiah.

They begin by dressing him like a king. For royal garments, they put a scarlet robe around him—scarlet being the color worn by Roman military, by high-ranking officials, and by the emperor himself.[5] For a diadem, they weave a crown of thorns together and place it on his head. For a scepter, they place a reed in his right hand, symbolizing a king's authority.

Yet, this costume that the soldiers force on Jesus is only cruel sarcasm. They proceed in their scoffing by kneeling before him and acting as if they are paying him homage. They even mimic the royal address one would give to the emperor—"Hail, Caesar!"—by saying to the scourged, condemned, and humiliated Jesus, "Hail, King of the Jews!"

Christians will see a great irony in this scene. While the soldiers scoff at Jesus, they have no idea how appropriate their words actually are. Despite their cruel intentions, they unwittingly proclaim the truth of Jesus Christ: He really is the Messiah, the true King of the Jews. The homage these pagan soldiers pay in jest anticipates the sincere honor countless gentiles will give Jesus as they worship him as their Lord and King. Most ironically, the soldiers, who in their mockery kneel before Jesus, will find themselves in the same position of reverence at the last judgment, when the words of St. Paul will be fulfilled: "that at the name of Jesus *every knee should bow*, in heaven and on earth and under the earth, and every tongue confess that Jesus Christ is Lord, to the glory of God the Father" (Phil 2:10-11).

But now the soldiers' mockery turns into physical abuse. The immature battalion begins to spit at him, slap him on the face, and strike his head with a rod (see Mt 27:30; Jn 19:3). Just as the chief priests mocked Jesus, slapped him and spit in his face during his trial before the Sanhedrin, so now the Romans get in on the act by taunting Jesus and inflicting him with similar forms of violence. One might hear echoes of Isaiah's prophecy about the suffering servant of the Lord: "I gave my back to the smiters, and my cheeks to those who pulled out the beard [that is, those who insulted me]; I hid not my face from shame and spitting" (Is 50:6).

The King's Enthronement
This is not the only scene from Christ's passion that carries royal overtones. Consider how so many of the events leading up to Christ's death are filled with regal imagery. During the trial Pilate asks Jesus, "Are you the *king* of the Jews?" (Mt 27:11). Pilate later presents Jesus to the crowds, saying, "Here is your *king!*" When the people request that Jesus be crucified, Pilate asks them, "Shall I crucify your *king?*" (Jn 19:14-15). At the crucifixion Pilate orders a sign to be placed over Christ's cross that says: "This is Jesus *the King* of the Jews" (Mt 27:37). While on the cross, the chief priests, scribes, and elders mock him: "He is *the King* of Israel; let him come down now from the cross, and we will believe

in him" (Mt 27:42). And shortly before Jesus dies, the "good thief" crucified alongside him says, "Jesus, remember me when you come in your *kingly* power" (Lk 23:42).

Thus when the ridiculing soldiers crown Jesus with thorns, dress him in royal colors, kneel before him and mockingly say, "Hail, *King* of the Jews!" this scene represents just one of the many instances in which the Gospels emphasize the kingship themes surrounding the story of Christ's passion and death.

From a human perspective, however, this seems to be an odd time to highlight Christ's royal majesty. How could Jesus be a triumphant king when he is stripped, scourged, beaten, mocked, and nailed to a cross? Christ's death seems like a humiliating defeat, not a royal triumph!

Yet, by stressing Christ's kingship precisely in his passion and death, the Gospels boldly proclaim the mystery of the cross. The cross is not a sign of defeat. Rather, it is the greatest victory the world has ever known. It is there on Calvary that Jesus establishes his kingdom by conquering sin and death through his redeeming sacrifice on our behalf. In this sense the crucifixion really is Christ's enthronement as King. Through his passion, death, and resurrection, Jesus defeats the devil and invites us to enter into the kingdom of God, sharing in his reign over sin and death.

The Fourth Sorrowful Mystery:
The Carrying of the Cross
Luke 23:26-31

Roman crucifixions generally took place outside the city walls along crowded roads, so that many people could witness what happened when someone revolted against Rome. At the crucifixion site the vertical part of the cross was implanted into the ground. The condemned criminal was given the crossbeam in the city and had it placed over his shoulders like a yoke, with his arms hooked over it. He would be forced to carry it through the streets and out the city gates.

It would be highly unusual for the Romans to permit another person to carry the crossbeam for a criminal condemned to crucifixion. Yet that is exactly what happens with Jesus in this fourth sorrowful mystery.

Simon of Cyrene

"And as they led him away, they seized one Simon of Cyrene, who was coming in from the country, and laid on him the cross, to carry it behind Jesus" (Lk 23:26).

Who is this Simon of Cyrene? And why is he forced to carry Christ's cross?

The fact that the Romans broke from the normal practice of having the criminal carry his own cross indicates just how beaten Jesus must have been from his scourging. He is so physically weak that the soldiers fear he may not even make it to the execution site outside the city. Roman soldiers had authority to require assistance from civilians, and they press into service Simon of Cyrene to carry Jesus' cross.

We do not know much about this Simon. The Gospels tell us he was from the North African city of Cyrene, which was a center of Jewish population in the region. He may have been in Jerusalem as a pilgrim for the Passover feast. It is also possible that Simon was a settler in the city, since devout Jews from Cyrene stayed in Jerusalem and there was a synagogue for Cyrenians there (see Acts 6:9).

Luke's Gospel notes that Simon is "coming in from the country" when he is enlisted to carry Jesus' cross. He probably has no idea about the dramatic events occurring in Jerusalem that day. The fact that he was not in Jerusalem during the uproar surrounding Christ's trial and condemnation tells us that he did not participate in the mob shouting for Jesus' execution. Not all of the Jews are so intensely opposed to Jesus.

On entering the city gates Simon would hear the riotous crowd coming toward him down a narrow Jerusalem street. Some are wailing in mourning, while others probably are shouting insults. He would see Roman soldiers pushing a staggering man who is barely able to carry a crossbeam. Finding himself engulfed in this tumultuous procession to a crucifixion, Simon is suddenly singled out by the Roman soldiers. They take the crossbeam off of the condemned man, put it on Simon's shoulders, and force him to carry Jesus' cross.

Luke notes that Simon carries the cross *behind* Jesus, symbolic of Christ's teaching about discipleship: "If any man would come after me, let him deny himself and *take up his cross* daily and *follow me*" (Lk 9:23). While it is true that Simon carried Christ's cross by compulsion, a tradition arose that this encounter with the cross of Jesus transformed him and that he and his family eventually became Christian. Some point to a verse in Mark's Gospel to support this tradition. Mark's account of this scene mentions that Simon has two sons, Alexander and Rufus (see Mk 15:21). This Rufus might be the well-known Christian Rufus in the Roman Church, whom Paul later calls "eminent in the Lord" (Rom 16:13)—indeed, the only other Rufus mentioned in the New Testament.

From Majesty to Mourning
"And there followed him a great multitude of the people, and of women who bewailed and lamented him" (Lk 23:27).

Ironically, Jesus rode majestically into Jerusalem on a colt earlier that week, with a "whole multitude" of disciples rejoicing and blessing him as "the King who comes in the name of the Lord" (Lk 19:37-38). Now he exits the holy city, humiliated and scourged, with "a great multitude" of people mourning his crucifixion. The weeping and lamenting of the women echo the prophecy of Zechariah 12:10: "And I will pour out on the house of David and the inhabitants of Jerusalem a spirit of compassion and supplication, so that, when they look on him whom they have pierced, they shall mourn for him, as one mourns for an only child, and weep bitterly over him, as one weeps over a first-born." Nevertheless, even their compassionate tears may not be enough to prevent the judgment that will come upon this city which is killing the Messiah.

Blessed Are the Barren?

"But Jesus turning to them said, 'Daughters of Jerusalem, do not weep for me, but weep for yourselves and for your children. For behold, the days are coming when they will say, "Blessed are the barren, and the wombs that never bore, and the breasts that never gave suck!" Then they will begin to say to the mountains, "Fall on us"; and to the hills, "Cover us." For if they do this when the wood is green, what will happen when it is dry?'" (Lk 23:28-31).

What provoked such a harsh beatitude from Jesus—"Blessed are the barren, and the wombs that never bore"? Especially within the ancient Jewish context, barrenness was a woman's greatest nightmare. Why would Jesus dare to call it a blessing?

Christ is starkly warning the women of what will happen to Jerusalem if it does not repent. When Jesus foretells how people will ask the mountains and hills to fall on them, he is alluding to Hosea's prophecy of judgment on Samaria: "They shall say to the mountains, Cover us, and to the hills, Fall upon us" (Hos 10:8). Just as the kingdom

of Samaria persisted in their rebellion against God and was destroyed
by a foreign army, so will Jerusalem be demolished unless it changes its
ways and repents for its leaders who are having Israel's Messiah killed.
In this way, Christ warns of the destruction of Jerusalem in A.D. 70,
when Roman armies will devastate the city with war, famine, and fire.

The Dry Wood

We can see this even more when Jesus leaves the weeping women with
the cryptic remark, "For if they do this when the wood is green, what
will happen when it is dry?" (Lk 23:31).

Green wood is moist and not able to be used in a fire, while dry
wood burns rather easily. With this imagery, Jesus is saying that he is
like green wood—innocent and not deserving of such harsh punishment. If Jesus is suffering such a horrible death under the Romans as
an innocent man, imagine the type of suffering the guilty in Jerusalem
will face when real revolutionaries rebel against Roman authority.

Indeed, much of Jerusalem will be burned like dry wood as
Roman forces squash the Jewish uprising in the generation after
Jesus. There will be so much devastation that Jesus can speak of
women wishing they were barren instead of having to see their children suffer such atrocities in Jerusalem's fiery destruction. That is
why Jesus says, "Do not weep for me, but weep for yourselves and
for your children." As one commentator put it, "The youngsters
playing in the streets in Jesus' day would become the firebrands of
the next generation, and would suffer the terrible consequences [of
the Roman armies]. The mothers should save their tears for when
they would really be needed."[6]

The Fifth Sorrowful Mystery:

The Crucifixion

Matthew 27:35-66; Mark 15:25-47; Luke 23:33-56; John 19:18-42

The Romans used crucifixion as punishment for the most serious of crimes, especially that of revolting against Roman rule. This form of punishment was so abhorrent that the ancient Roman orator Cicero once said the mere mention of the word *cross* "should be far removed not only from the person of a Roman citizen but from his thoughts, his eyes, and his ears."[7]

The goal of crucifixion was not simply to execute but to do so with the maximum amount of pain and public humiliation. Men condemned to this type of death were stripped of their clothes and nailed or bound to a cross with their arms extended and raised. Thus immobilized, their exposed bodies had no means of coping with heat, cold, insects, or pain.

Since crucifixion did not damage any vital organ or cause excessive bleeding, death came slowly, sometimes over several days as the weight of the unsupported body gradually caused the breathing muscles to give in to fatigue. Eventually the crucified man succumbed to shock or asphyxiation. Sometimes a man was given a footrest at the bottom of the vertical beam. This, however, was no act of mercy. It simply enabled the crucified man to lift himself up for a breath and thus survive in agonizing pain for an even longer period of time.

This most severe form of punishment sent a powerful message to the Jews: Don't even think about rising up against us. Consequently, the cross stood as one of the greatest symbols of Jewish suffering under the curse of Roman domination. It is precisely into this suffering that Israel's Messiah enters as he is crucified on Calvary.

"Father, Forgive Them"

"And when they came to the place which is called The Skull, there they crucified him, and the criminals, one on the right and one on the left. And Jesus said, 'Father, forgive them; for they know not what they do'" (Lk 23:33-34).

Although crucifixion is intended to take away every vestige of a criminal's freedom and dignity, the Gospels show us that Jesus is no ill-fated victim. He emerges on the cross as one who is still on a mission. He is still in control, trusting in the Father and carrying out his redemptive plan.

First, consider how the cross does not inhibit Christ's ministry of mercy. Indeed, from there he performs the most powerful act of forgiveness one could offer—forgiving one's enemies. Despite the fact that the Jewish leaders have slapped him, the Roman battalion has scourged him, and now the soldiers have crucified him, Jesus responds to these horrendous acts with love by showing mercy even to his executioners. Though he has been falsely accused, wrongly ridiculed, and unjustly tortured, Jesus, in the midst of his riveting pain on the cross, shows sympathy and understanding for those who are killing him: "Father, forgive them; for they know not what they do."

Notice how Jesus not only forgives but even makes excuses for his executioners, giving them the benefit of the doubt. He understands that these people would not be putting him to death if they truly realized what they were doing. Thus Jesus embodies his teaching to love those who have injured us: "Love your enemies, do good to those who hate you, bless those who curse you, pray for those who abuse you" (Lk 6:27-28).

As the *Catechism* explains, we are called to imitate Christ's merciful response to evils committed against us—to turn injuries into intercessory prayer for those who hurt us. "It is not in our power not to feel or to forget an offense; but the heart that offers itself to the Holy Spirit turns injury into compassion and purifies the memory in transforming the hurt into intercession" (*CCC*, 2843).

"You Will Be With Me in Paradise"

"One of the criminals who were hanged railed at him, saying, 'Are you not the Christ? Save yourself and us!' But the other rebuked him, saying, 'Do you not fear God, since you are under the same sentence of condemnation? And we indeed justly; for we are receiving the due reward of our deeds; but this man has done nothing wrong.' And he said, 'Jesus, remember me when you come in your kingly power.' And he said to him, 'Truly, I say to you, today you will be with me in Paradise'" (Lk 23:39-43).

Here we see a second example of how the nails cannot keep Jesus from carrying out his saving mission. Even while facing his own death on the cross, Jesus grants salvation to the dying, repentant criminal.

After the Jewish leaders and Roman soldiers mock Jesus for claiming to be Israel's Messiah-King (see Lk 23:35-36), one of the criminals with Jesus joins in the jeering: "Are you not the Christ? Save yourself and us!" The other crucified man, however, rebukes the first. Humbly, he admits his own guilt and recognizes that Jesus is innocent and undeserving of this cruel punishment. He turns to Jesus and says, "Remember me when you come in *your kingly power*."

The good thief's words are remarkable. Unlike everyone else who is mocking Jesus, this man does not think Christ's death is a defeat but rather anticipates in it the beginning of the kingdom. This criminal thus is the first to recognize that the cursed Roman cross upon which Jesus hangs is actually the means by which Christ's kingdom will be established. He sees that Jesus' crucifixion is somehow his enthronement as the king.

Jesus responds to this man's great faith and last-minute conversion by granting him far more than he requested. Jesus does not simply promise to remember him when he enters into his kingdom, but he announces this man's imminent salvation: *"Today* you will be with me in Paradise"* (Lk 23:43).

"Behold, Your Mother"

"When Jesus saw his mother, and the disciple whom he loved standing near, he said to his mother, 'Woman, behold, your son!' Then he said to the disciple, 'Behold, your mother!' And from that hour the disciple took her to his own home" (Jn 19:26-27).

Standing near the cross, Mary watches her son suffer this most horrible of deaths. She can do nothing to help him or even comfort him. Simeon's words from the Presentation come to fulfillment: "A sword will pierce through your own soul also" (Lk 2:35).

Now, in the last moments of his life, just before he says, "It is finished," Jesus performs one more act of kindness on the cross. He entrusts his mother to "the beloved disciple," John. On a basic level, this act will provide care for Mary after he dies. On another level, however, bringing Mary and the beloved disciple into a mother-son relationship has profound theological meaning as well. As many Catholics throughout the centuries have seen, Jesus is not just showing concern for his mother but is actually entrusting all Christians, who are represented by the beloved disciple, to her maternal care.

In John's Gospel certain characters represent not only individuals in the narrative but also larger groups. For example, Nicodemus, the Pharisee who meets Jesus at night and does not understand Christ's message, represents the many Pharisees who have difficulty understanding and accepting Christ's mission (see Jn 3:1-21). The Samaritan woman who meets Jesus at the well is an individual who undergoes a conversion, but she also represents the many Samaritans who will come to believe in Christ (see Jn 4:1-42). Similarly, "the beloved disciple" in John's Gospel is the individual apostle John who also represents all faithful Christians.

"The Beloved Disciple"

In John's Gospel we see that the beloved disciple is the one who shares a close intimacy with Jesus at the Last Supper (see Jn 13:23), remains with Jesus during his crucifixion (see Jn 19:26), is the first to believe in the risen Lord (see Jn 20:8), and continues to bear testimony to Jesus (see Jn 21:7, 20, 24). In other words, "the beloved disciple" is an ideal follower of Christ. As the model disciple in John's Gospel, this individual also represents all faithful Christian disciples.

This is why Catholics have seen in this action at the cross a basis for understanding Mary's spiritual motherhood of all Christians. Since the beloved disciple represents all faithful followers of Christ, Mary, who becomes the mother of the beloved disciple in this scene, becomes also the mother of all the faithful Christians he represents. As John Paul II comments, "The Mother of Christ, who stands at the very center of this mystery—a mystery which embraces each individual and all humanity—is given as mother to every single individual and all mankind. The man at the foot of the Cross is John, 'the disciple whom he loved.' But it is not he alone. Following tradition, the [Second Vatican] Council does not hesitate to call Mary 'the Mother of Christ and mother of mankind.'... Indeed she is 'clearly the mother of the members of Christ ... since she cooperated out of love so that there might be born in the Church the faithful.' "[8]

"Why Have You Abandoned Me?"

"Now from the sixth hour there was darkness over all the land until the ninth hour. And about the ninth hour Jesus cried with a loud voice, 'Eli, Eli, lama sabach-thani?' that is, 'My God, my God, why hast thou forsaken me?'" (Mt 27:45-46).

On the cross Jesus enters into the depths of Israel's sufferings and the pains of all humanity as he takes on the sins of the world. Many have interpreted his words, "My God, my God, why hast thou forsaken me?" as a cry of despair, signifying his alienation from the Father who has rejected the Son on Calvary. Yet on closer examination we can see that Jesus is quoting the opening line from Psalm 22, which is not a psalm of despair but a hymn of tremendous hope in times of intense trial.

The psalmist experiences such hardship that he feels *as if* God has abandoned him: "My God, my God, why hast thou foresaken me? Why art thou so far from helping me, from the words of my groaning? O my God, I cry by day, but thou dost not answer; and by night, but find no rest" (Ps 22:1-2).

The psalm goes on to describe the righteous man's sufferings in ways that foreshadow Christ's crucifixion. For example, it says "But I am a worm, and no man; scorned by men, and despised by the people. All who seek me *mock at me*, they make mouths at me, *they wag their heads*; 'He committed his cause to the Lord; let him deliver him*, let him rescue him, for he delights in him'" (Ps 22:6-8).

These verses anticipate the events on Calvary. There people pass by the crucified Christ, "wagging their heads" and scoffing at him while the Jewish leaders almost repeat the words of the psalm, saying, "He trusts in God; let God deliver him now, if he desires him" (Mt 27:43).

Psalm 22 also foreshadows the type of physical suffering Christ endures: "They have *pierced my hands and feet*—I can count all my bones—they stare and gloat over me; they *divide my garments* among them, and for my raiment they *cast lots*" (Ps 22:16-18). These verses are fulfilled when the Roman soldiers pierce Jesus by nailing him to the cross and then divide his garments among them by casting lots (see Mt 27:35).

Confidence on the Cross

Yet, however terrible the psalmist's sufferings may be, Psalm 22 ultimately expresses the righteous man's great hope in the face of severe trial. In the midst of being persecuted and beaten, and feeling as if God is far away, the psalmist still trusts that the Lord will hear his plea and rescue him. He recalls how the Lord has answered the cry of the righteous throughout history and trusts that God will hear him and come to his aid as well: "Yet thou art holy, enthroned on the praises of Israel. In thee our fathers trusted; they trusted, and thou didst deliver them. To thee they cried, and were saved" (Ps 22:3-5). He then calls on the Lord as his only source of strength: "Be not far from me, for trouble is near and there is none to help" (Ps 22:11).

The psalm concludes with a resounding confidence that God will vindicate him and all those who suffer for righteousness' sake:

I will tell of thy name to my brethren;
in the midst of the congregation I will praise thee:
You who fear the Lord, praise him!
all you sons of Jacob, glorify him,
and stand in awe of him, all you sons of Israel!
For he has not despised or abhorred the affliction of the afflicted;
and he has not hid his face from him,
but has heard, when he cried to him.
From thee comes my praise in the great congregation;

my vows I will pay before those who fear him.
The afflicted shall eat and be satisfied;
those who seek him shall praise the Lord!
May your hearts live for ever!

PSALM 22:22-26

This is not the cry of a man in utter despair. It is the voice of a man who entrusts himself to the Lord. He praises the God who hears the cries of the afflicted, and he has firm confidence that the Lord will rescue him. The psalmist even foretells how, in this vindication of the righteous, God's reign will extend to all nations: "All the ends of the earth shall remember and turn to the Lord; and all the families of the nations shall worship before him. For dominion belongs to the Lord, and he rules over the nations" (Ps 22:27-28).

In quoting the first line of Psalm 22—"My God, my God, why have you forsaken me?"—Jesus would be invoking the whole context of this psalm. Since the psalm expresses trust in God and ends on a clearly victorious note, ancient Jews would not interpret Christ's words as a cry of despair.

Certainly Jesus expresses his union with us in the depths of our suffering and sin. At the same time, however, his reference to Psalm 22 expresses his total trust that the Father will vindicate him over his enemies. Thus Christ's cry on Good Friday anticipates his victory on Easter Sunday, when he will rise from the dead and restore us as sons and daughters of the Father. Indeed, through Christ's resurrection, the high point of Psalm 22 will be fulfilled: God will reign over all the earth, rescuing all who suffer and bringing "all the families of the nations" together to worship before him (Ps 22:27).

SIX

Scriptural Reflections on the Glorious Mysteries

John Paul II says the five Glorious Mysteries invite us to look beyond the darkness of Good Friday and contemplate the glory of Christ's resurrection and ascension. In the first mystery Jesus rises triumphant over sin, death, and all that keeps us from union with God. Then in the second mystery he ascends in glory to the right hand of the Father, where he reigns over heaven and earth.

In the third mystery, the descent of the Holy Spirit on Pentecost, we arrive at the hinge of the Glorious Mysteries. Here we reflect on how Christ's work of salvation in his resurrection and ascension is applied to our lives. Through Christ's Spirit dwelling in our hearts, we share in the life of the risen and ascended Jesus. This supernatural life in Christ through the Spirit transforms us in such a profound way that we are reconciled with God as adopted sons and daughters. In Christ we can truly call God Father. As St. Paul says, "God has sent the Spirit of his Son into our hearts, crying, 'Abba! Father!'" (Gal 4:6).

The last two glorious mysteries present the preeminent member of the Church who has been completely filled with the Holy Spirit and already shares in the fullness of Christ's glory: Mary. When we look at her splendor in heaven, we see an icon of what awaits us if we imitate her faithfulness and allow Christ's Spirit to transform our lives. In the Assumption we contemplate Mary's "enjoying beforehand, by a unique privilege, the destiny reserved for all the just at the resurrection of the dead."[1] In the last glorious mystery, we ponder Mary being crowned as Queen of heaven and earth. While contemplating Mary's participation in her son's reign, we are reminded of our own royal mission to reign with Christ over sin and death for the rest of eternity.

The First Glorious Mystery:
The Resurrection
Matthew 28:1-15; Mark 16:1-18; Luke 24:1-49; John 20:1–21:25

On the sabbath they rested according to the commandment. But on the first day of the week, at early dawn, they went to the tomb, taking the spices which they had prepared. And they found the stone rolled away from the tomb.

LUKE 23:56–24:2

Mary Magdalene and the other holy women go to the tomb of Jesus at the crack of dawn. These are the women who remained with him during his final hours on Calvary. They witnessed his body being taken down from the cross, wrapped in fine linen, and quickly laid in a tomb before the Sabbath rest began that evening.

Now it is the Sunday morning after Jesus died, and the Sabbath has ended. These same faithful women will be the first to return to the tomb. They are in mourning, and they bring spices so they can anoint the body that had been buried hastily on Good Friday. They have no idea that they are about to become the first witnesses to the most important event in the history of the world.

The Empty Tomb

Upon their arrival the women discover that the large stone that enclosed the tomb has been rolled away. Matthew's Gospel explains what has happened overnight: "There was a great earthquake; for an angel of the Lord descended from heaven and came and rolled back the stone" (Mt 28:2). The angel's appearance "was like lightning and his raiment white as snow" and it threw the Roman soldiers who guarded the tomb into a state of shock. "And for fear of him the guards trembled and *became like dead men*" (Mt 28:4). Notice the irony: The very ones who were supposed to be guarding the tomb of a dead man have now become like dead men themselves, while the body of the crucified Christ has risen.

However, the women do not understand all this yet. At least from the perspective of Luke's Gospel, they only know that the large stone has been moved from the doorway and that the tomb is now open. Imagine their surprise when they walk into the tomb. Expecting to find the corpse of Jesus, the women instead discover two men "in dazzling apparel," angels of the Lord (Lk 24:4-6; see Acts 1:10).

Amazed at all that has taken place this early morning—the rolled-away stone, the missing body, and now two angels appearing—the women respond in fear, bowing their faces to the ground before the heavenly messengers. The angels quickly address the women's bewilderment about the missing body: "Why do you seek the living among the dead? He is not here, but has risen" (Lk 24:5).

Still Brothers

The women's realization of Christ's resurrection reaches a climax when they see the risen Lord himself. On their way back from the tomb, Mary Magdalene and "the other Mary" (Mary the mother of James) become the first to encounter the resurrected Jesus.

"They departed quickly from the tomb with fear and great joy...

And behold, Jesus met them and said, 'Hail!' And they came up and took hold of his feet and worshiped him. Then Jesus said to them, 'Do not be afraid; go and tell my brethren to go to Galilee, and there they will see me'" (Mt 28:8-10).

The truth of the Resurrection is now confirmed by their seeing the risen Christ for themselves. In awe, the women grasp his feet—an expression of homage one would give to a king. The only way they can respond to the resurrected Jesus is to fall down at his feet and worship him.

What is perhaps most striking in this scene is that Jesus calls the apostles "my brethren." Even though they abandoned him on Good Friday, Jesus still views the apostles as his brothers. We can see this even more clearly when Christ appears to the apostles for the first time later that day.

An Unexpected Peace

"On the evening of that day, the first day of the week, the doors being shut where the disciples were, for fear of the Jews, Jesus came and stood among them and said to them, 'Peace be with you.' When he had said this, he showed them his hands and his side. Then the disciples were glad when they saw the Lord. Jesus said to them again, 'Peace be with you'" (Jn 20:19-21).

Christ's first words to the frightened, cowardly apostles in hiding are "Peace be with you." This is no pious throw-away line, nor a simple greeting. In the biblical Hebrew understanding, peace—*shalom*—means right relationships. It is not simply about avoiding war and fighting. Going much deeper, *shalom* signifies harmonious friendship, covenant intimacy, a relationship of trust.

The risen Christ comes to offer the apostles this *shalom*. Perhaps he greets the apostles with these words to make it clear that he has risen not to issue condemnation and vengeance upon them but to bring them forgiveness and assurance of his friendship.

This is astonishing. Think about what has happened between Jesus and the apostles in the seventy-two hours leading up to Easter. After sharing the Passover, these closest friends of Jesus could not stay awake and pray with him in his moment of greatest agony in the garden. When he was arrested, these men abandoned him. When the crowds condemned Jesus to death, none of these men came to his defense. When he was carrying his cross, they were nowhere to be found. In their cowardice, all but one let their master die on his own. A greater sense of disloyalty and abandonment could hardly be imagined.

Yet Jesus says to these failed men, "Peace be with you." In offering them forgiveness, Jesus does not simply sweep everything under the rug. He does not say, "I'm OK, you're OK. It's no big deal." Instead he seeks them out in their hiding, comes behind their closed doors, and reminds them of their tragic decisions on Good Friday: he shows them the nail marks in his hands and the piercing from the lance in his side. Jesus will not let them run away from that.[2] They must come to terms with the awful truth about their actions and lack of action, about what they have done and what they have failed to do. And it is precisely in this humbling moment of the apostles' facing their weaknesses and failings that Jesus meets them and offers them forgiveness and a restored friendship. He offers them *shalom*.

Behind Closed Doors

This scene highlights what may be one of the most unique aspects of Christianity. While a number of modern religious trends focus on man's search for God, Christianity is much more about God's search for us. Just as he did on Easter Sunday, Jesus continuously seeks us out whenever we push him to the side of our lives or run away from him.

Sometimes we may hide from God's call or close doors in our hearts, afraid to let Jesus fully into certain areas of our lives. But he will not let us stay in hiding for long. Sooner or later he will allow us to experience the emptiness, anxiety, and unhappiness that come from a life not centered on him. He will allow us to face our fears, brokenness, and failings.

Jesus wants to pass through the doors and meet us there in the dark crevices of our existence—in our insecurities, our doubts, our weaknesses, and our sins. He wants us to come to terms with what we have done and what we have failed to do. He wants us to face the truth about who we really are.

Yet he comes not to point fingers and condemn. He comes to offer forgiveness, healing, and a new way of life in him. He comes to offer *shalom*.

The Mystery of Easter

This is simply the pattern of salvation found in the mission of the Son of God, who descended into our fallen humanity in order to heal us and raise us up to share in his divinity. In the Incarnation the Almighty God descended to earth and became a man, entering the broken human family. Throughout his public ministry the all-holy Son of God continued to lower himself, journeying to the darkest corners of Israel. He did not stay in the temple with the religious elite but associated with the lepers, the sick, the prostitutes, and other sinners. By speaking with them, touching them, and sharing meals with them, Jesus united himself to the outcasts of first-century Judaism. By meeting them in their lowest points, he healed them, forgave them, and restored them to covenant relationship with the Father.

This descent of God is seen especially on Good Friday. On the cross we encounter most vividly the mystery of the God who relentlessly seeks out his people when they have run away. On Calvary we see that he searches for us even to the point of descending into the depths of our sufferings, sinfulness, and estrangement from the Father. And it is precisely there that he finds us. By meeting us at this lowest point of our existence, Jesus, the Son of God who is perfectly united to the Father, is able to transform our weak, fallen humanity and lift it up with him in his resurrection. The all-holy Son of God unites himself to our utter brokenness on Good Friday so he can raise us up with him on Easter Sunday. In the Resurrection, Jesus offers the fallen human family a restored relationship with the Father. Indeed, the risen Christ offers us *shalom.*

The Second Glorious Mystery:

The Ascension

Acts 1:1-11; Mark 16:19-20; Luke 24:50-53

To them he presented himself alive after his passion by many proofs, appearing to them during forty days, and speaking of the kingdom of God.

ACTS 1:3

This verse from Acts sets the context for Christ's ascension. It is significant that Jesus has been appearing to the apostles and talking to them about the kingdom for *forty days* after his resurrection. For the ancient Israelites, the number forty would symbolize a time of intense training and preparation for some great work. It recalls, for example, the forty years Israel spent in the desert preparing to enter the Promised Land and the forty days Moses fasted on Mount Sinai when receiving the Ten Commandments.

Most of all, these forty days parallel Jesus' fast in the desert before he was led by the Spirit to begin proclaiming the kingdom in Galilee (see Lk 4:14). In the same way he now spends forty days preparing the apostles to be led by the Holy Spirit at Pentecost, when they will begin their ministry to the ends of the earth.

The Kingdom Question

"So when they had come together, they asked him, 'Lord, will you at this time restore the kingdom to Israel?'" (Acts 1:6).

The apostles ask an excellent question. After all, if Jesus is the son of David and the Messiah-King, it would be expected that he would be the one to rebuild the Davidic dynasty, which has been lying in ruins for centuries. Although foreign powers have controlled the people of Israel for much of the last six hundred years, the prophets foretold that the kingdom eventually would be reconstituted and become even more glorious than it was in the days of David and Solomon. Not only would it reunite Israel, but it also would gather all peoples to worship the one true God. Indeed, this future kingdom would reign over all the earth.

At the Last Supper Jesus spoke of this renewed Israel and of the apostles playing a leadership role in it (see Lk 22:29-30). Now, after having spent forty days in training with the resurrected King talking about the kingdom, the apostles are anxiously waiting for their mission to begin. That is why they ask if now is the time for the kingdom to be restored.

To the End of the Earth

"He said to them, 'It is not for you to know times or seasons which the Father has fixed by his own authority. But you shall receive power when the Holy Spirit has come upon you; and you shall be my witnesses

in Jerusalem and in all Judea and Samaria and to the end of the earth'"
(Acts 1:7-8).

At first glance it may seem as if Jesus is avoiding the apostles' question when he says "It is not for you to know times or seasons...." However, although he does not reveal the precise timing of the kingdom's restoration, he does affirm its coming and calls on the apostles to play a crucial role in its expansion. In fact, in these words Jesus gives the apostles their marching orders. He tells them they will be his witnesses "in *Jerusalem* and in all *Judea* and *Samaria* and to the *end of the earth.*"

On one level these words provide an itinerary for their mission and an outline for the rest of the Acts of the Apostles: Their proclamation of the kingdom will begin in *Jerusalem* (see Acts 2–7), move out to the regions of *Judea* and *Samaria* (see Acts 8–12), and then spread throughout much of the known world, even to the capital city of Rome (see Acts 13–28).

On another level, by announcing the apostles' mission to go out to all the nations, Jesus answers their kingdom question. He says that *they* will be the ones to fulfill the worldwide mission of the kingdom. In fact, the kingdom will be restored and its universal reign extended precisely through their own witness to the gospel from Jerusalem to the ends of the earth.

A Cloud of Glory

"And when he had said this, as they were looking on, he was lifted up, and a cloud took him out of their sight. And while they were gazing into heaven as he went, behold, two men stood by them in white robes, and said, 'Men of Galilee, why do you stand looking into heaven? This Jesus, who was taken up from you into heaven, will come in the same way as you saw him go into heaven'" (Acts 1:9-11).

Jesus ascends to heaven on no ordinary cloud from the sky but on the magnificent cloud of God's glory. Many times throughout salvation history God has manifested his divine presence to Israel in the form of a cloud. It was in a cloud of glory that God's presence filled the sanctuary in the desert, filled the temple in Jerusalem, and overshadowed Christ during his transfiguration. Now that same cloud of glory lifts Jesus up and brings him to heaven in triumphant glory (see 1 Tm 3:16).

Christ's return to the Father on a cloud also signals the fulfillment of an important prophecy from the Old Testament. The prophet Daniel had a vision of a "son of man" figure who appeared victorious over his enemies and was carried to God *on the clouds of heaven* in order to be given a world-wide kingdom that would last forever:

"I saw in the night visions, and behold, with the clouds of heaven there came one like a son of man, and he came to the Ancient of Days and was presented before him. And to him was given dominion and glory and kingdom, that all peoples, nations, and languages should serve him; his dominion is an everlasting dominion, which shall not pass away, and his kingdom one that shall not be destroyed" (Dn 7:13-14).

With Christ being lifted into heaven on a cloud, the ascension scene represents a fulfillment of Daniel's prophecy. Jesus is the "son of man" who in his exaltation is presented before God the Father, the Ancient of Days, and is given an everlasting kingdom that will reign over all nations (see *CCC,* 664). As such, Christ's ascension may provide a further response to the apostles' question, "When will the kingdom be restored to Israel?" By rising to the Father on a cloud of glory, Jesus confirms that he is the Son of Man who has emerged victorious and that the restored kingdom Daniel envisioned has finally arrived. It is now up to the apostles to extend this kingdom to the ends of the earth.

Our Mission

Like the first apostles, we, too, share in the mission of spreading Christ's kingdom in the world today. Yet we do not have to become a missionary in Africa to do this. Whether a teacher in the classroom, a businessman in the workplace, a college student on campus, or a mother raising children in the home, all Christians play a crucial role in helping build the kingdom in the specific areas where God has called them to serve. By bringing the extraordinary witness of Christian truth, virtue, and love into our ordinary, daily endeavors, we can help transform our culture into the kingdom of the risen and ascended Christ.

It is true that the apostles were charged to go out to the end of the earth, but they had to start with their own people, right in their own capital city of Jerusalem. We, too, do not have to look very far to find places where the truth of the Gospel and Christ's love are desperately needed. Let us imitate the apostles and begin our mission right in our own country, bringing Christ into our workplaces, our parishes, our schools, our neighborhoods, and most of all, our own homes.

The Third Glorious Mystery:
The Descent of the Holy Spirit
Acts 2:1-41

When the day of Pentecost had come, they were all together in one place.
ACTS 2:1

Pentecost originally was not a Christian feast but a Jewish one. Each year, on the fiftieth day after Passover, the Jews celebrated Pentecost as an agricultural festival in which many would make a pilgrimage to Jerusalem to offer the "first fruits" from the wheat harvest.

Eventually Pentecost took on greater theological meaning as they began to associate it with the giving of the Law at Mount Sinai. On this mountain God gave the people the Ten Commandments and established Israel as his covenant people. According to the Book of Exodus, they arrived at Mount Sinai about a month and a half after the first Passover in Egypt (see Ex 12:1-3; 19:1). Since the Jews celebrated Pentecost each year at roughly the same time period after Passover, this feast day began to commemorate the giving of the covenant at Sinai and the founding of Israel as God's chosen people.

This background helps us understand what the apostles are doing in Jerusalem. They are gathered together for the Jewish Feast of Pentecost (see Acts 2:1). It also helps us appreciate how fitting it is that God chose to send the Holy Spirit to the apostles on *this* particular day. Just as Pentecost celebrated the beginning of the old covenant with Israel, so now this day marks the start of the new covenant era with the Church.

A New Sinai

"And suddenly a sound came from heaven like the rush of a mighty wind, and it filled all the house where they were sitting. And there appeared to them tongues as of fire, distributed and resting on each one of them. And they were all filled with the Holy Spirit and began to speak in other tongues, as the Spirit gave them utterance" (Acts 2:2-4).

This scene of the Holy Spirit falling upon the apostles on the mountain of Jerusalem is reminiscent of the way God appeared to the Israelites on another famous mountain, Mount Sinai. Just before giving the Ten Commandments, the Lord descended on Sinai in the form of *fire*. This was accompanied by the *loud sound* of a trumpet blast and God's speaking to Moses in thunder (see Ex 19:16-19). Furthermore, at least one strand of Jewish tradition describes God communicating to the Israelites at Sinai through fire in a *language familiar to the people.* Commenting on this scene, Philo of Alexandria, a first-century Jewish writer, said: "And a voice sounded forth out of the midst of the fire which had flowed from heaven, a most marvelous and awful voice, the flame being endowed with articulate speech in a language familiar to the hearers, which expressed its words with such clearness and distinctness that the people seemed rather to be seeing than hearing it."[3]

This seems to parallel what happens when the Holy Spirit comes upon the apostles in Jerusalem on Pentecost.[4] Just as the old covenant was established at Sinai about a month and a half after the first Passover lambs were sacrificed in Egypt, so now the new covenant is established with the Church about a month and a half after the true Passover Lamb was sacrificed on the cross. And just as God descended on Mount Sinai in the form of fire, with a loud sound and with divine speech familiar to the people, so now God's Holy Spirit descends on the mountain of Jerusalem with the extraordinary signs of *fire,* a *loud sound,* and *miraculous speech that is understood by people of different languages.* Portrayed as a new Sinai event, the descent of the Holy Spirit at Pentecost marks another turning point in salvation history, the birth of the new covenant people of God, the Church.

A New Kind of Law

Nevertheless, amidst these many parallels we can see that what is given in the new covenant (the Holy Spirit) far surpasses what was given in the old covenant (the Law). Even though Israel received the Ten Commandments at Sinai, the rest of the Old Testament story clearly shows that the nation constantly failed to keep it. The lesson we learn from the Scriptures is that the Law by itself is not enough.

And if we are honest, most of us realize this from our own personal experience. Simply *knowing* what is right does not always mean we will *do* what is right. How many times have we known we should do something good but failed to do it? How many times have we known we should avoid saying or doing something but find ourselves saying or doing it anyway? With St. Paul we can humbly admit our utter weakness: "I do not understand my own actions. For I do not do what I want, but I do the very thing I hate.... For I do not do the good I want, but the evil I do not want is what I do" (Rom 7:15, 19).

The problem is not simply that people do not know the Law but that they cannot keep the Law on their own power. This is why the prophets foretold that God would establish a new covenant with a new kind of law: a law that would be written on people's hearts. This new law would do much more than inform people of a moral code they should follow. It would actually give people a supernatural strength to rise above their weak, fallen human nature and walk in God's ways.

The Book of Jeremiah, for example, describes the contrast between the old law, which Israel broke, and the interior law, which would come in the new covenant era:

"Behold, the days are coming, says the Lord, when I will make a new covenant with the house of Israel and the house of Judah, not like the covenant which I made with their fathers when I took them by the hand to bring them out of the land of Egypt, my covenant which they broke... But this is the covenant which I will make with the house of Israel after those days, says the Lord: I will put my law within them, and I will write it upon their hearts; I will be their God, and they shall be my people" (Jer 31:31-33).

What is important for our reflection on the descent of the Holy Spirit at Pentecost is that the prophet Ezekiel associates this new law with God's own Spirit dwelling in us, transforming our hard hearts and strengthening us to follow God's ways: "A new heart I will give you, and a new spirit I will put within you; and I will take out of your flesh the heart of stone and give you a heart of flesh. And I will put my spirit within you, and cause you to walk in my statutes" (Ez 36:26-27).

Changing Our Hearts of Stone

With the Holy Spirit descending on the people at Pentecost, this third glorious mystery stands as a fulfillment of Jeremiah's and Ezekiel's prophecies about the new covenant. While the old law was written by the finger of God on tablets of stone, the new law is written by God's Holy Spirit on the hearts of believers, prompting them to love as Christ loved, turning them away from sin, and giving them the power to fulfill the law, which they could not keep on their own (see 2 Cor 3:3; Rom 8:1-4; *CCC*, 733–36).

This gift of Pentecost, the indwelling of the Holy Spirit, makes all the difference in the world. Indeed, with Christ's Spirit we can love our God, our spouse, our children, our coworkers, and our friends in a way that rises above our own selfish, proud, fearful human nature. When Christ's Spirit works through us, his generosity transforms our selfishness, his humility softens our pride, and his courage overcomes our timidity. When we allow the Holy Spirit to change our hearts of stone and permeate our lives in this way, we can truly say, "It is no longer I who live, but Christ who lives in me" (Gal 2:20).

A Reversal of Babel

"Now there were dwelling in Jerusalem Jews, devout men from every nation under heaven. And at this sound the multitude came together, and they were bewildered, because each one heard them speaking in his own language. And they were amazed and wondered, saying, 'Are not all these who are speaking Galileans? And how is it that we hear, each of us in his own native language?'" (Acts 2:5-8).

Jews and gentile converts to Judaism from all over the Roman Empire are gathered in Jerusalem for Pentecost (see Acts 2:5-10). Expecting simply to participate in this Jewish pilgrimage feast, they end up experiencing much more than they ever imagined. They witness the descent of the Holy Spirit and become some of the first converts to Christianity.

Filled with the Holy Spirit, Peter delivers his first sermon, proclaiming the death and resurrection of the Messiah. At the end of his speech he challenges the people: "Repent, and be baptized every one of you in the name of Jesus Christ for the forgiveness of your sins; and you shall receive the gift of the Holy Spirit" (Acts 2:38). About three thousand come to believe in the gospel and are baptized that day (see Acts 2:41).

Pentecost serves as a preview of things to come. Many from this international gathering of Jews and gentile converts hear the gospel, believe, and are baptized on Pentecost. This scene in Jerusalem, however, anticipates what will happen across the world. Many Jews and gentiles throughout the Roman empire will hear the gospel preached by the apostles. They, too, will believe, be baptized, and be gathered into Christ's Church.

Moreover, the fact that each person hears the apostles in his or her own language may signal the reversal of the curse of the Tower of Babel and the reunion of the human family. In Genesis 11 God diversified the human languages so people could no longer understand each other's speech, signifying the division within the human family sown by sin. The descent of the Holy Spirit, however, overcomes that language barrier at Pentecost. This scene thus signifies that the new law of the Spirit overcomes sin and that the fractured human family is being reunited in the one family of God, the Church.

Mary's Prayer for Pentecost

"All these with one accord devoted themselves to prayer, together with the women and Mary the mother of Jesus, and with his brethren" (Acts 1:14).

We close this reflection on the third glorious mystery by considering Mary's role in it. The Acts of the Apostles notes that the mother of Jesus was gathering with the apostles to pray in the period leading up to Pentecost (see Acts 1:14). Vatican II describes Mary's prayer in these days as a petition for the whole Church to receive the same Holy Spirit that already overshadowed her at the Annunciation.[5]

In commenting on this theme, John Paul II once said that Mary's prayer attracts the action of the Holy Spirit in the world. With Mary's "yes" at the Annunciation, the Holy Spirit conceived the physical body of Christ in her womb. Now, with Mary's prayerful intercession at Pentecost, the same Spirit descends upon the apostles to form the Mystical Body of Christ, the Church.[6]

Mary's intercession continues to foster the coming of the Holy Spirit in our lives today. Through her maternal care for all Christians, she pleads for that new law of the Spirit to be written deep in our hearts, permeating all our thoughts, desires, words, and actions. May Mary continue to implore Christ's Spirit to transform our weak, self-centered human nature with his infinite, supernatural love.

The Fourth Glorious Mystery:
The Assumption of Mary
Psalm 132:8; Luke 1:28; Revelation 12:1

What does Catholicism teach about the Assumption of Mary? And why is this event contemplated in the fourth glorious mystery? Let us begin by considering a few key points from the *Catechism of the Catholic Church* (see *CCC*, 966).

First, in discussing the Assumption, the *Catechism* affirms that Mary did not suffer from original sin, but was conceived full of grace. According to this doctrine known as the Immaculate Conception, God's supernatural life dwelt in Mary from the very beginning of her existence.

It is important to emphasize that from a Catholic perspective, the Immaculate Conception is not simply about Mary. This doctrine, which has its roots in early Christianity, ultimately is about the mystery of Jesus Christ. God became man in Mary's womb. Since Jesus truly is the all-holy God, the second Person of the Trinity, Catholics believe he is worthy to dwell in a pure vessel, a holy temple. Thus it is fitting that God would prepare Mary as an immaculate dwelling place for the God-man. It seems appropriate for God to enter humanity in the womb of a woman who was full of grace and not stained by sin.

The Annunciation scene in Luke's Gospel may at least point in this direction. The angel Gabriel greets Mary, "Hail, full of grace." The Greek word in Luke's Gospel for "full of grace" (Lk 1:28) is in a perfect passive participle form, which would indicate that Mary *already* has been filled with God's saving grace, even before Jesus was conceived in her womb.[7] As we will see, the Immaculate Conception will serve as a basis for understanding Mary's assumption.

Mary's Death?

Second, the *Catechism* teaches Mary was taken to heaven when the course of her earthly life was finished. The Church does not declare whether Mary died and then was assumed into heaven or whether she was assumed before she died. It leaves open both possibilities. However, the majority of theologians and saints throughout the centuries affirm that Mary *did* experience death—not as a penalty for sin but in conformity to her son, who himself willingly experienced death on our behalf. In support of this latter view, John Paul II said, "The Mother is not superior to the Son who underwent death, giving it a new meaning and changing it into a means of salvation."[8]

Third, the *Catechism* affirms Mary was taken up body and soul into heavenly glory. One of the consequences of original sin is the corruption of the body (see *CCC*, 400; Gn 3:19). If Mary was full of grace and did not suffer from original sin, it is fitting that she, like her son, would not experience such bodily corruption. Therefore the Church affirms that Mary was taken "body and soul" into heavenly glory right at the end of her earthly life.

Biblical Assumptions

Although there are no explicit "proof texts" in Scripture for Mary's assumption, some biblical themes may at least shed light on this doctrine. For example, the notion of being taken up into heaven has some precedent in Scripture. Enoch was taken into heaven without seeing death (see Heb 11:5), and Elijah was whisked into heaven by the chariots of fire at the end of his life (see 2 Kg 2:11). If God could assume these righteous men of the Old Testament, it is certainly possible that Jesus could assume his own mother as well.

Even more, since the Bible presents Mary as the first Christian disciple, it is fitting that she would be the first to receive the blessings of following Christ. In the New Testament, Mary is presented as the first to hear God's word and accept it at the Annunciation (see Lk 1:38, 45). In the visitation, she responds to God's word promptly by going in haste to help Elizabeth. She also describes herself as a servant of the Lord (see Lk 1:38, 48). Mary remains faithful to her son, following him even to the cross (see Jn 19:25-27), where she experiences the fulfillment of Simeon's prophecy at the Presentation: "A sword will pierce through your own soul also" (Lk 2:35). She perseveres in faith throughout her life, gathering with the apostles for prayer even after her son's ascension (see Acts 1:14). Thus the New Testament presents a clear overall portrait of Mary as the first and preeminent disciple of Christ, who hears the word of God and keeps it in her heart.

Since one of the blessings promised to all faithful disciples is victory over death, it is fitting that Mary, who is the first and model disciple of Christ, would be the first to receive this blessing. Catholics thus believe the privilege of resurrection promised to all faithful Christians was given first to Mary and in a totally unique way. While the rest of us hope to have our bodies raised to glory at the end of time, Mary experienced the resurrection and glorification of her body at the moment her earthly life ended. Thus her assumption—which flows from her unique participation in Christ's victory as the mother of the Savior and as the first and most faithful of Christ's followers—anticipates to some degree our own share in the fullness of that victory if we persevere as followers of Christ.

The Saints and Scripture

Theologians and saints throughout the centuries have seen other Scripture passages and themes as shedding light on Mary's assumption. While numerous examples could be considered, let us look briefly at just a few texts Pope Pius XII highlighted in his proclamation of Mary's Assumption in 1950.[9]

He notes how some have turned to Psalm 132, which celebrates the ark of the covenant being brought by David to the temple in Jerusalem: "Arise, O Lord, and go to thy resting place, thou and the ark of thy might" (Ps 132:8). Since Mary is like a new ark of the covenant carrying God's presence in her womb, some have seen these words as prefiguring Mary's assumption. Just as David transferred the ark to find rest in the Jerusalem temple of old, so now Jesus, the true son of David, brings Mary, the new ark of the covenant, to her final resting place in heaven. Moreover, some have looked upon "the Ark of the Covenant, built of incorruptible wood and placed in the Lord's temple, as a type of the most pure body of the Virgin Mary, preserved and exempted from all the corruption of the tomb and raised up to such glory in heaven."[10]

Pope Pius XII also notes how others interestingly have turned to the fourth commandment, "Honor your father and your mother" (Ex 20:12), as a source for understanding Mary's assumption. These would say that if Jesus observed the fourth commandment perfectly, he would honor his mother by assuming her into heaven at the end of her life. Along similar lines, St. Francis de Sales once said, "What son would not bring his mother back to life and would not bring her into paradise after her death if he could?"[11]

Another text commonly used to shed light on Mary's assumption is Revelation 12:1, which presents "a woman clothed with the sun" appearing in heaven as a sign.[12] In this apocalyptic vision the woman gives birth to a male child who is described as the Messiah, ruling all nations with a rod of iron and carried up to the throne of God (see Rv 12:5; Ps 2:9). While we will treat this passage more in our reflection on the fifth glorious mystery, we can say here that since the male child is generally understood to be the Messiah, the woman giving birth to this child can be seen as referring to Mary. With the woman being "clothed with the sun" and appearing in heaven, Catholics often have seen in this vision support for Mary's assumption, by which she was clothed in God's glory and began her heavenly reign.

An Event of Love

Finally, let us consider what a moment the Assumption must have been for Mary! In describing this scene, some of the Church Fathers spoke of Jesus himself coming back to earth to take his mother and bring her to her heavenly home. More recently, John Paul II has said that the Assumption truly was an event of love, in which Mary's ardent longing to be with her son was finally fulfilled. In fact, many paintings of the Assumption portray Mary in this way—rising in splendor on a cloud to heaven, received by the angels with trumpets and celebration, and reunited joyfully with her beloved son.

While artistic depictions of this triumphant event in Mary's life are often celebrated, not as well-known are the many pieces of art that portray her last moments on earth just before her assumption. Yet just such a depiction of the end of Mary's life—her moment between heaven and earth—can be found on one of the main doors of St. Peter's Basilica in Rome. There Mary is surprisingly portrayed as *falling*, as if she were definitively letting go of all the trials and sufferings of this life and allowing herself to fall asleep. Indeed, she is letting go of life itself as she passes from this world to the next. It is just at this moment of abandoning herself into the Father's hands that the angels rush down to catch her and bring her up to heaven.

This depiction captures an aspect of Mary's assumption that offers us hope in the midst of our trials throughout this "valley of tears." This is the hope that God will carry us through our distress and lift up our heavy hearts. With Mary's intercession, may we learn to let go of the many burdens, troubles, and worries that wear us down in this world and entrust ourselves to God's loving care. May we like Mary fall into the Father's arms, so that he may support us in our present sufferings and raise us to himself on the last day.

The Fifth Glorious Mystery:
The Crowning of Mary
Luke 1:43; Revelation 12:1

For many Christians today, it is not obvious why Mary should be called a queen. After all, she is not the wife of Christ the King but his mother. Yet from a biblical perspective Mary's queenship would make a lot of sense.

In the ancient Near East the woman sitting on the throne in the kingdom was not the king's wife but his mother. Most kings in this period had large harems. King Solomon, for example, had seven hundred wives and three hundred concubines (see 1 Kg 11:3). It would have been impossible to bestow the queenship on a thousand women! Yet, while the king might have had multiple wives, he only had one mother; thus the queenship was given to her.

The Scriptures attest to the important role of the queen mother in ancient Israel. In the Kingdom of Judah she held an official position in the royal court, participating in her son's reign over the people. She was described as having a throne and a crown (see 1 Kg 2:19; Jer 13:18) and serving as a counselor to her royal son (see Prv 31:1). The queen mother was one of the first mentioned in the list of palace officials (see 2 Kg 24:12), and in the narrative of 1 and 2 Kings she almost always is introduced by name whenever a new king assumed the throne in Judah. Most of all, the queen mother served as an advocate for the people, receiving petitions from the people and presenting them to her royal son (see 1 Kg 2:19).

A Royal Advocate

We can see the importance of the queen mother by contrasting two scenes in the life of Bathsheba: her role when she was simply the wife of King David and her role as queen mother when her son Solomon assumed the throne. When her husband David was still the king and Bathsheba entered the royal chamber, she had to bow with her face to the ground and pay him homage, saying, "May my lord King David live for ever" (1 Kg 1:16, 31).

We find a very different picture once Bathsheba's son Solomon becomes king and she steps into the office of queen mother. A man named Adonijah recognizes Bathsheba's powerful position as advocate and asks her to bring a petition for him to her royal son. Knowing that the king always listens to the intercession of the queen mother, Adonijah confidently says to her, "Pray ask King Solomon—*he will not refuse you*" (1 Kg 2:17).

Bathsheba agrees to bring the petition to the king. However, when she enters the royal chamber this time as queen mother, her experience is entirely different compared to the last time she was there. Instead of Bathsheba having to pay homage to the king, King Solomon stands up and bows down before *her*. Even more, the king has a throne brought for her at his right hand, symbolizing her position of authority. When Bathsheba says she has a petition to present to Solomon, he responds, "Make your request, my mother; for I will not refuse you" (1 Kg 2:19-20). With these words Solomon affirms his commitment to the queen mother's intercessory role as advocate in the kingdom.[13]

"Mother of My Lord"

All this is important background to understanding the royal office of the mother of Christ. Jesus is the new son of David, the Messiah-King who fulfills all the promises given to the Davidic kingdom. If in the

Jewish, biblical worldview of the Davidic kingdom the king's mother reigned as queen, then the mother of the new Davidic king, Jesus, clearly would be understood as the new queen mother.

That seems to be what Elizabeth affirms in the visitation scene. Filled with the Holy Spirit, she greets the mother of Jesus, saying, "Why is this granted me, that the mother of my Lord should come to me?" (Lk 1:43). The title Elizabeth bestows on Mary is charged with royal significance. In the royal court language of the ancient Near East, the title "mother of my Lord" would have been used to address the queen mother, for "my lord" was a title of honor for the king himself (2 Sm 24:21). Therefore, in calling Mary "mother of my Lord" Elizabeth acknowledges her as the mother of the king—in other words, as queen mother.

A Woman Clothed With the Sun

Another passage that sheds light on Mary's royal office is found in the Book of Revelation, chapter 12:

"And a great portent appeared in heaven, a woman clothed with the sun, with the moon under her feet, and on her head a crown of twelve stars;... She brought forth a male child, one who is to rule all the nations with a rod of iron, but her child was caught up to God and to his throne" (Rv 12:1, 5).

Who is this mysterious woman appearing in such royal splendor, clothed with the sun, with the moon under her feet, and crowned with twelve stars? The key to unlocking the mystery of this queenly woman can be found in the identity of the child she bears. Revelation 12 tells us that the woman gives birth to a male child who "rules all the nations with a rod of iron" (Rv 12:5).

This description of the child is significant because it is taken directly from the messianic Psalm 2. In this psalm God foretells how he will rescue the Messiah-King from his enemies and establish for him a reign over all the earth: "Ask of me, and I will make *the nations* your heritage, and the ends of the earth your possession. You shall break them with a rod of iron" (Ps 2:8-9). Since the Book of Revelation portrays the male-child with this messianic imagery from Psalm 2, the child would be seen as the long-awaited Messiah-King.

Once the child is identified as the Messiah, the question becomes then, who is the royal woman who gave birth to the Messiah? Clearly that woman is Mary.[14]

In Revelation 12 Mary appears in all her majesty, reigning in heaven alongside her royal son. Indeed, she is the queen mother of Christ's everlasting kingdom. Like the queen mothers of old, she wears a crown on her head, symbolizing her regal office. The twelve stars on her crown express her reign over the Church, which is born from the twelve tribes of Israel and founded on the twelve apostles. Clothed with the sun, she radiates God's glory. With the moon under her feet, she appears in royal authority, since "under the feet" imagery symbolized regal power and defeat of one's enemies (see Ps 8:6; 110:1).

Finally, the combination of the sun, moon, and stars imagery may recall the famous dream of the patriarch Joseph. In this vision, Joseph saw the sun, moon, and eleven stars bowing down before him (see Gn 37:9). This dream foreshadowed how Joseph would rule over his father, mother, and eleven brothers when he rose to the second highest position in Pharoah's kingdom in Egypt. The similar images describing Mary in Revelation 12 may highlight her own royal authority as she assumes one of the most important offices in Christ's kingdom, that of the queen mother.

"I Will Not Refuse You"

With all this background we are still left wondering, what does Mary's queenship *mean*? Is this a throwback to an outdated governmental structure? Is her queenship simply a figurehead position?

To understand Mary's royal office, we must view it from within the biblical perspective of Christ's kingdom, not secular monarchies. Jesus himself emphasized that his kingdom "is not of this world" (Jn 18:36). Unlike the pagan rulers who use their authority to serve themselves, Jesus said he exercises his authority "not to be served but to serve" (Mt 20:28).

Mary, the faithful servant of the Lord, participates in his kingdom in this same way. Indeed, in Christ's kingdom, to serve is to reign. And Mary reigns as queen by serving as a royal advocate for God's people. Like the queen mothers in the Davidic kingdom, Mary stands as a powerful intercessor for the people in Christ's kingdom today.

John Paul II pointed out that Mary lovingly presents our needs and petitions before Christ's throne and so serves the kingdom by leading souls closer to her son: "Thus, far from creating distance between her and us, Mary's glorious state as queen brings about a continuous and caring closeness. She knows everything that happens in our lives and supports us with maternal love in our trials. Taken up to heavenly glory, Mary dedicates herself totally to the work of salvation. She wants every living person to know the happiness granted to her. She is a queen who gives all that she possesses, participating above all in the life and love of Christ."[15]

In this last mystery of the rosary let us give thanks for the loving intercession of Mary, our queen mother. May we confidently turn to Mary with our needs, knowing that she presents our petitions before her royal son and trusting that Jesus responds to her as Solomon did to Bathsheba, saying, "Make your request, my mother; for I will not refuse you" (1 Kg 2:20).

SEVEN

A Scriptural Rosary

This section provides readers with a practical tool to help incorporate more Scripture in their praying of the rosary. In what is commonly known as a "scriptural rosary," we offer for each mystery ten short lines from the Bible.

As we saw in chapter two, John Paul II encourages us to begin each decade of the rosary with a reading from Scripture. This helps prepare our minds to contemplate the particular mystery at hand. The biblical verses in this scriptural rosary can serve as a resource to help nourish our contemplation. One or two verses given here can be recited out loud or reflected on quietly at the start of each decade.

Having ten Scripture verses for each decade at one's disposal may help free the mind from worrying about locating a mystery in the Bible every time an "Our Father" bead approaches. Also, since there are ten verses available, different aspects of the mystery can be chosen for reflection each time the rosary is prayed.

Another way these verses can be used is to pray a traditional scriptural rosary itself. In this practice, one Bible verse is read before the recitation of each Hail Mary. For example, in the first joyful mystery, the Annunciation, the first Scripture verse is read: "In the sixth month the angel Gabriel was sent from God ..." Then the first Hail Mary is recited. Next, a second Biblical verse from the Annunciation is read before the second Hail Mary is recited, and so on throughout each decade.

This approach has similarities with the way the rosary was sometimes prayed originally—with one meditation point from Christ's life being contemplated with each Hail Mary (as discussed in chapter one).

Selecting only ten short lines from Scripture for each of the mysteries is a challenging task. Some were chosen, while other inspiring ones were left out. In order to draw the connection between this scriptural rosary and the rest of this book, the verses discussed in the biblical reflections on the mysteries in chapters three through six were given priority. Those reflections, therefore, help illumine the scriptural rosary which follows.

Finally, it must be said that there are many ways one could present a scriptural rosary, and the particular model offered here in no way is meant to be all-encompassing. It is simply intended to serve as a tool that an individual, family, or group could use in whatever way best helps them encounter the mysteries of the rosary in Sacred Scripture.

The First Joyful Mystery
The Annunciation

1. In the sixth month the angel Gabriel was sent from God to ... a virgin betrothed to a man whose name was Joseph ... and the virgin's name was Mary (Lk 1:26-27). *Hail Mary ...*

2. And he came to her and said, "Hail, full of grace, the Lord is with you!" (Lk 1:28). *Hail Mary ...*

3. But she was greatly troubled at the saying, and considered in her mind what sort of greeting this might be (Lk 1:29). *Hail Mary ...*

4. And the angel said to her, "Do not be afraid, Mary, for you have found favor with God" (Lk 1:30). *Hail Mary ...*

5. "And behold, you will conceive in your womb and bear a son, and you shall call his name Jesus" (Lk 1:31). *Hail Mary ...*

6. "He will be great, and will be called the Son of the Most High;... and he will reign over the house of Jacob for ever" (Lk 1:32-33). *Hail Mary ...*

7. And Mary said to the angel, "How can this be, since I have no husband?" (Lk 1:34). *Hail Mary ...*

8. And the angel said to her, "The Holy Spirit will come upon you, and the power of the Most High will overshadow you" (Lk 1:35). *Hail Mary ...*

9. "Therefore the child to be born will be called holy, the Son of God" (Lk 1:35). *Hail Mary ...*

10. "Behold, I am the handmaid of the Lord; let it be to me according to your word" (Lk 1:38). *Hail Mary ...*

The Second Joyful Mystery
The Visitation

1. In those days Mary arose and went with haste into the hill country, to a city of Judah, and she entered the house of Zechariah and greeted Elizabeth (Lk 1:39-40). *Hail Mary ...*

2. And when Elizabeth heard the greeting of Mary, the babe leaped in her womb (Lk 1:41). *Hail Mary ...*

3. Elizabeth was filled with the Holy Spirit and she exclaimed with a loud cry, "Blessed are you among women, and blessed is the fruit of your womb!" (Lk 1:41-42). *Hail Mary ...*

4. "And why is this granted me, that the mother of my Lord should come to me?" (Lk 1:43). *Hail Mary ...*

5. "For behold, when the voice of your greeting came to my ears, the babe in my womb leaped for joy" (Lk 1:44). *Hail Mary ...*

6. "And blessed is she who believed that there would be a fulfillment of what was spoken to her from the Lord" (Lk 1:45). *Hail Mary ...*

7. And Mary said, "My soul magnifies the Lord, and my spirit rejoices in God my Savior" (Lk 1:46-47). *Hail Mary ...*

8. "For he has regarded the low estate of his handmaiden" (Lk 1:48). *Hail Mary ...*

9. "For behold, henceforth all generations will call me blessed" (Lk 1:48). *Hail Mary ...*

10. "For he who is mighty has done great things for me, and holy is his name" (Lk 1:49). *Hail Mary ...*

The Third Joyful Mystery
The Nativity

1. And Joseph also went up from Galilee,... to the city of David, which is called Bethlehem ... to be enrolled with Mary his betrothed, who was with child (Lk 2:4-5). *Hail Mary ...*
2. And she gave birth to her first-born son and wrapped him in swaddling cloths and laid him in a manger, because there was no place for them in the inn (Lk 2:7). *Hail Mary ...*
3. And in that region there were shepherds out in the field, keeping watch over their flock by night (Lk 2:8). *Hail Mary ...*
4. And an angel of the Lord appeared to them, and the glory of the Lord shone around them, and they were filled with fear (Lk 2:9). *Hail Mary ...*
5. And the angel said to them, "Be not afraid; for behold, I bring you good news of a great joy ... for to you is born this day in the city of David a Savior, who is Christ the Lord" (Lk 2:10-11). *Hail Mary ...*
6. And suddenly there was with the angel a multitude of the heavenly host praising God and saying, "Glory to God in the highest, and on earth peace among men with whom he is pleased" (Lk 2:13-14). *Hail Mary ...*
7. And they went with haste, and found Mary and Joseph, and the babe lying in a manger (Lk 2:16). *Hail Mary ...*
8. Now when Jesus was born ... wise men from the East came to Jerusalem, saying, "Where is he who has been born king of the Jews? For we have seen his star in the East, and have come to worship him" (Mt 2:1-2). *Hail Mary ...*
9. And going into the house they saw the child with Mary his mother, and they fell down and worshiped him (Mt 2:11). *Hail Mary ...*
10. But Mary kept all these things, pondering them in her heart (Lk 2:19). *Hail Mary ...*

The Fourth Joyful Mystery
The Presentation of Jesus

1. And when the time came for their purification ... they brought him up to Jerusalem to present him to the Lord (Lk 2:22). *Hail Mary* ...

2. Now there was a man ... whose name was Simeon, and this man was ... looking for the consolation of Israel (Lk 2:25). *Hail Mary* ...

3. And it had been revealed to him by the Holy Spirit that he should not see death before he had seen the Lord's Christ (Lk 2:26). *Hail Mary* ...

4. When the parents brought in the child Jesus,... [Simeon] took him up in his arms and blessed God (Lk 2:27-28). *Hail Mary* ...

5. [Simeon] said, "Lord, now lettest thou thy servant depart in peace, according to thy word" (Lk 2:28-29). *Hail Mary* ...

6. "For mine eyes have seen thy salvation which thou hast prepared in the presence of all peoples, a light for revelation to the Gentiles, and for glory to thy people Israel" (Lk 2:30-32). *Hail Mary* ...

7. Simeon blessed them and said to Mary his mother, "Behold, this child is set for the fall and rising of many in Israel, and for a sign that is spoken against" (Lk 2:34). *Hail Mary* ...

8. "And a sword will pierce through your own soul also" (Lk 2:35).

9. And there was a prophetess, Anna.... She did not depart from the temple, worshiping with fasting and prayer night and day (Lk 2:36-37). *Hail Mary* ...

10. And coming up at that very hour she gave thanks to God, and spoke of him to all who were looking for the redemption of Jerusalem (Lk 2:38). *Hail Mary* ...

The Fifth Joyful Mystery
The Finding of the Child Jesus in the Temple

1. Now his parents went to Jerusalem every year at the feast of the Passover.... And when the feast was ended, as they were returning, the boy Jesus stayed behind in Jerusalem (Lk 2:41, 43). *Hail Mary ...*

2. His parents did not know it, but supposing him to be in the company they went a day's journey (Lk 2:43-44). *Hail Mary ...*

3. They sought him among their kinsfolk and acquaintances; and when they did not find him, they returned to Jerusalem, seeking him (Lk 2:44-45). *Hail Mary ...*

4. After three days they found him in the temple, sitting among the teachers, listening to them and asking them questions (Lk 2:46). *Hail Mary ...*

5. All who heard him were amazed at his understanding and his answers. And when [Mary and Joseph] saw him they were astonished (Lk 2:47-48). *Hail Mary ...*

6. His mother said to him, "Son, why have you treated us so? Behold, your father and I have been looking for you anxiously" (Lk 2:48). *Hail Mary ...*

7. And he said to them, "How is it that you sought me? Did you not know that I must be in my Father's house?" (Lk 2:49). *Hail Mary ...*

8. And they did not understand the saying which he spoke to them (Lk 2:50). *Hail Mary ...*

9. And he went down with them and came to Nazareth, and was obedient to them (Lk 2:51). *Hail Mary ...*

10. His mother kept all these things in her heart (Lk 2:51). *Hail Mary ...*

The First Luminous Mystery
Christ's Baptism in the Jordan

1. In those days came John the Baptist, preaching in the wilderness of Judea, "Repent, for the kingdom of heaven is at hand" (Mt 3:1-2). *Hail Mary* ...

2. Then went out to him Jerusalem and all Judea and all the region about the Jordan (Mt 3:5). *Hail Mary* ...

3. They were baptized by him in the river Jordan, confessing their sins (Mt 3:6). *Hail Mary* ...

4. [John said], "I baptize you with water for repentance, but he who is coming after me is mightier than I;... He will baptize you with the Holy Spirit and with fire" (Mt 3:11). *Hail Mary* ...

5. Then Jesus came from Galilee to the Jordan to John, to be baptized by him (Mt 3:13). *Hail Mary* ...

6. John would have prevented him, saying, "I need to be baptized by you, and do you come to me?" (Mt 3:14). *Hail Mary* ...

7. But Jesus answered him, "Let it be so now; for thus it is fitting for us to fulfil all righteousness" (Mt 3:15). *Hail Mary* ...

8. And when Jesus was baptized, he went up immediately from the water, and behold, the heavens were opened (Mt 3:16). *Hail Mary* ...

9. He saw the Spirit of God descending like a dove, and alighting on him (Mt 3:16). *Hail Mary* ...

10. Lo, a voice from heaven, saying, "This is my beloved Son, with whom I am well pleased" (Mt 3:17). *Hail Mary* ...

The Second Luminous Mystery
The Wedding Feast at Cana

1. On the third day there was a marriage at Cana in Galilee, and the mother of Jesus was there; Jesus also was invited to the marriage, with his disciples (Jn 2:1-2). *Hail Mary ...*
2. When the wine failed, the mother of Jesus said to him, "They have no wine" (Jn 2:3). *Hail Mary ...*
3. And Jesus said to her, "O woman, what have you to do with me? My hour has not yet come" (Jn 2:4). *Hail Mary ...*
4. His mother said to the servants, "Do whatever he tells you" (Jn 2:5). *Hail Mary ...*
5. Now six stone jars were standing there, for the Jewish rites of purification, each holding twenty or thirty gallons (Jn 2:6). *Hail Mary ...*
6. Jesus said to them, "Fill the jars with water." And they filled them up to the brim (Jn 2:7). *Hail Mary ...*
7. He said to them, "Now draw some out, and take it to the steward of the feast." So they took it (Jn 2:8). *Hail Mary ...*
8. When the steward of the feast tasted the water now become wine, and did not know where it came from,... the steward of the feast called the bridegroom (Jn 2:8-9). *Hail Mary ...*
9. [The steward] said to him, "Every man serves the good wine first; and when men have drunk freely, then the poor wine; but you have kept the good wine until now" (Jn 2:10). *Hail Mary ...*
10. This, the first of his signs, Jesus did at Cana in Galilee, and manifested his glory; and his disciples believed in him (Jn 2:11). *Hail Mary ...*

The Third Luminous Mystery
The Proclamation of the Kingdom

1. Jesus spoke to them, saying, "I am the light of the world; he who follows me will not walk in darkness, but will have the light of life" (Jn 8:12). *Hail Mary ...*

2. In him [Jesus] was life, and the life was the light of men. The light shines in the darkness, and the darkness has not overcome it. (Jn 1:4-5). *Hail Mary ...*

3. Jesus came into Galilee, preaching the gospel of God, and saying, "The time is fulfilled, and the kingdom of God is at hand; repent, and believe in the gospel" (Mk 1:14-15). *Hail Mary ...*

4. "Therefore do not be anxious, saying, 'What shall we eat?' or 'What shall we drink?' or 'What shall we wear?' For the Gentiles seek all these things; and your heavenly Father knows that you need them all" (Mt 6:31-32). *Hail Mary ...*

5. "But seek first his kingdom and his righteousness, and all these things shall be yours as well" (Mt 6:33). *Hail Mary ...*

6. And Jesus went about all the cities and villages, teaching in their synagogues and preaching the gospel of the kingdom, and healing every disease and infirmity (Mt 9:35). *Hail Mary ...*

7. And behold, they brought to him a paralytic, lying on his bed; and when Jesus saw their faith he said to the paralytic, "Take heart, my son; your sins are forgiven" (Mt 9:2). *Hail Mary ...*

8. Jesus looked up and said to [the woman caught in adultery], "Woman, where are they? Has no one condemned you?" She said, "No one, Lord" (Jn 8:10-11). *Hail Mary ...*

9. And Jesus said, "Neither do I condemn you; go, and do not sin again" (Jn 8:11). *Hail Mary ...*

10. [Jesus] said to [the apostles], "Receive the Holy Spirit. If you forgive the sins of any, they are forgiven; if you retain the sins of any, they are retained" (Jn 20:22-23). *Hail Mary ...*

The Fourth Luminous Mystery
The Transfiguration

1. And after six days Jesus took with him Peter and James and John his brother, and led them up a high mountain apart (Mt 17:1). *Hail Mary ...*
2. And he was transfigured before them, and his face shone like the sun (Mt 17:2). *Hail Mary ...*
3. His garments became white as light (Mt 17:2). *Hail Mary ...*
4. And behold, there appeared to them Moses and Elijah, talking with him (Mt 17:3). *Hail Mary ...*
5. And Peter said to Jesus, "Lord, it is well that we are here; if you wish, I will make three booths here, one for you and one for Moses and one for Elijah" (Mt 17:4). *Hail Mary ...*
6. He was still speaking, when lo, a bright cloud overshadowed them (Mt 17:5). *Hail Mary ...*
7. A voice from the cloud said, "This is my beloved Son, with whom I am well pleased; listen to him" (Mt 17:5). *Hail Mary ...*
8. When the disciples heard this, they fell on their faces, and were filled with awe (Mt 17:6). *Hail Mary ...*
9. But Jesus came and touched them, saying, "Rise, and have no fear" (Mt 17:7). *Hail Mary ...*
10. And when they lifted up their eyes, they saw no one but Jesus only (Mt 17:8). *Hail Mary ...*

The Fifth Luminous Mystery
The Institution of the Eucharist

1. Then came the day of Unleavened Bread, on which the passover lamb had to be sacrificed (Lk 22:7). *Hail Mary ...*

2. So Jesus sent Peter and John, saying, "Go and prepare the passover for us, that we may eat it" (Lk 22:8). *Hail Mary ...*

3. And when the hour came, he sat at table, and the apostles with him (Lk 22:14). *Hail Mary ...*

4. And he said to them, "I have earnestly desired to eat this passover with you before I suffer; for I tell you I shall not eat it until it is fulfilled in the kingdom of God" (Lk 2:15-16). *Hail Mary ...*

5. And he took a cup, and when he had given thanks he said, "Take this, and divide it among yourselves for I tell you that from now on I shall not drink of the fruit of the vine until the kingdom of God comes" (Lk 22:17-18). *Hail Mary ...*

6. And he took bread, and when he had given thanks he broke it and gave it to them, saying, "This is my body which is given for you" (Lk 22: 19). *Hail Mary ...*

7. "Do this in remembrance of me" (Lk 22:19). *Hail Mary ...*

8. And likewise the cup after supper, saying, "This cup which is poured out for you is the new covenant in my blood" (Lk 22:20). *Hail Mary ...*

9. So Jesus said to them,... "He who eats my flesh and drinks my blood has eternal life, and I will raise him up at the last day" (Jn 6:53-54). *Hail Mary ...*

10. "For my flesh is food indeed, and my blood is drink indeed. He who eats my flesh and drinks my blood abides in me, and I in him" (Jn 6:55-56). *Hail Mary ...*

The First Sorrowful Mystery
The Agony in the Garden

1. And he came out, and went, as was his custom, to the Mount of Olives; and the disciples followed him (Lk 22:39). *Hail Mary ...*

2. And when he came to the place he said to them, "Pray that you may not enter into temptation" (Lk 22:40). *Hail Mary ...*

3. And taking with him Peter and the two sons of Zebedee, he began to be sorrowful and troubled (Mt 26:37). *Hail Mary ...*

4. Then he said to them, "My soul is very sorrowful, even to death; remain here, and watch with me" (Mt 26:38). *Hail Mary ...*

5. And he withdrew from them about a stone's throw, and knelt down and prayed (Lk 22:41). *Hail Mary ...*

6. "Father, if thou art willing, remove this cup from me; nevertheless not my will, but thine, be done" (Lk 22:42). *Hail Mary ...*

7. And there appeared to him an angel from heaven, strengthening him (Lk 22:43). *Hail Mary ...*

8. And being in an agony he prayed more earnestly; and his sweat became like great drops of blood falling down upon the ground (Lk 22:44). *Hail Mary ...*

9. And when he rose from prayer, he came to the disciples and found them sleeping for sorrow, and he said to them, "Why do you sleep? Rise and pray that you may not enter into temptation" (Lk 22:45-46). *Hail Mary ...*

10. "Behold, the hour is at hand, and the Son of man is betrayed into the hands of sinners. Rise, let us be going; see, my betrayer is at hand" (Mt 26:45-46). *Hail Mary ...*

The Second Sorrowful Mystery
The Scourging at the Pillar

1. Now at the feast the governor was accustomed to release for the crowd any one prisoner whom they wanted (Mt 27:15). *Hail Mary ...*

2. And they had then a notorious prisoner, called Barabbas (Mt 27:16). *Hail Mary ...*

3. The governor again said to them, "Which of the two do you want me to release for you?" And they said, "Barabbas" (Mt 27:21). *Hail Mary ...*

4. Pilate said to them, "Then what shall I do with Jesus who is called Christ?" They all said, "Let him be crucified" (Mt 27:22). *Hail Mary ...*

5. So when Pilate saw that he was gaining nothing, but rather that a riot was beginning, he took water and washed his hands before the crowd (Mt 27:24). *Hail Mary ...*

6. [Pilate said], "I am innocent of this righteous man's blood; see to it yourselves" (Mt 27:24). *Hail Mary ...*

7. And all the people answered, "His blood be on us and on our children!" (Mt 27:25). *Hail Mary ...*

8. Then he released for them Barabbas, and having scourged Jesus, delivered him to be crucified (Mt 27:26). *Hail Mary ...*

9. But he was wounded for our transgressions, he was bruised for our iniquities (Is 53:5). *Hail Mary ...*

10. Upon him was the chastisement that made us whole, and with his stripes we are healed" (Is 53:5). *Hail Mary ...*

The Third Sorrowful Mystery
The Crowning With Thorns

1. And the soldiers led him away inside the palace (that is, the praetorium); and they called together the whole battalion (Mk 15:16). *Hail Mary ...*
2. And they clothed him in a purple cloak (Mk 15:17). *Hail Mary ...*
3. And plaiting a crown of thorns they put it on him (Mk 15:17). *Hail Mary ...*
4. [They] put a reed in his right hand (Mt 27:29). *Hail Mary ...*
5. And kneeling before him they mocked him, saying, "Hail, King of the Jews!" (Mt 27:29). *Hail Mary ...*
6. [They] struck him with their hands (Jn 19:3). *Hail Mary ...*
7. And they struck his head with a reed (Mk 15:19). *Hail Mary ...*
8. And [they] spat upon him (Mk 15:19). *Hail Mary ...*
9. And when they had mocked him, they stripped him of the purple cloak, and put his own clothes on him (Mk 15:20). *Hail Mary ...*
10. "I gave my back to the smiters;... I hid not my face from shame and spitting" (Is 50:6). *Hail Mary ...*

The Fourth Sorrowful Mystery
The Carrying of the Cross

1. And [the soldiers] led him out to crucify him (Mk 15:20). *Hail Mary ...*

2. And as they led him away, they seized one Simon of Cyrene, who was coming in from the country (Lk 23:26). *Hail Mary ...*

3. [They] laid on him the cross, to carry it behind Jesus (Lk 23:26). *Hail Mary ...*

4. And there followed him a great multitude of the people, and of women who bewailed and lamented him (Lk 23:27). *Hail Mary ...*

5. But Jesus turning to them said, "Daughters of Jerusalem, do not weep for me, but weep for yourselves and for your children" (Lk 23:28). *Hail Mary ...*

6. "For behold, the days are coming when they will say, 'Blessed are the barren, and the wombs that never bore, and the breasts that never gave suck!'" (Lk 23:29). *Hail Mary ...*

7. "Then, they will begin to say to the mountains, 'Fall on us'; and to the hills, 'Cover us'" (Lk 23:30). *Hail Mary ...*

8. "For if they do this when the wood is green, what will happen when it is dry?" (Lk 23:31). *Hail Mary ...*

9. And they brought him to the place called Golgotha (which means the place of a skull) (Mk 15:22). *Hail Mary ...*

10. And they offered him wine mingled with myrrh; but he did not take it (Mk 15:23). *Hail Mary ...*

The Fifth Sorrowful Mystery
The Crucifixion

1. And when they came to the place which is called The Skull, there they crucified him, and the criminals, one on the right and one on the left (Lk 23:33). *Hail Mary ...*

2. And Jesus said, "Father, forgive them; for they know not what they do" (Lk 23:34). *Hail Mary ...*

3. One of the criminals who were hanged railed at him, saying, "Are you not the Christ? Save yourself and us!" (Lk 23:39). *Hail Mary ...*

4. But the other rebuked him.... And he said, "Jesus, remember me when you come in your kingly power" (Lk 23:40, 42). *Hail Mary ...*

5. And he said to him, "Truly, I say to you, today you will be with me in Paradise" (Lk 23:43). *Hail Mary ...*

6. When Jesus saw his mother, and the disciple whom he loved standing near, he said to his mother, "Woman, behold, your son!" Then he said to the disciple, "Behold, your mother!" (Jn 19:26-27). *Hail Mary ...*

7. And about the ninth hour Jesus cried with a loud voice,... "My God, my God, why hast thou forsaken me?"(Mt 27:46). *Hail Mary ...*

8. After this Jesus, knowing that all was now finished, said (to fulfil the scripture), "I thirst" (Jn 19:28). *Hail Mary ...*

9. So they put a sponge full of the vinegar on hyssop and held it to his mouth. When Jesus had received the vinegar, he said, "It is finished" (Jn 19:29-30). *Hail Mary ...*

10. Then Jesus, crying with a loud voice, said, "Father, into thy hands I commit my spirit!" And having said this he breathed his last (Lk 23:46). *Hail Mary ...*

The First Glorious Mystery
The Resurrection

1. Now after the sabbath, toward the dawn of the first day of the week, Mary Magdalene and the other Mary went to see the sepulchre (Mt 28:1). *Hail Mary ...*

2. And they found the stone rolled away from the tomb, but when they went in they did not find the body (Lk 24:2-3). *Hail Mary ...*

3. While they were perplexed about this, behold, two men stood by them in dazzling apparel;... the men said to them, "Why do you seek the living among the dead? He is not here, but has risen" (Lk 24:4-5). *Hail Mary ...*

4. So they departed quickly from the tomb with fear and great joy, and ran to tell his disciples (Mt 28:8). *Hail Mary ...*

5. And behold, Jesus met them and said, "Hail!" And they came up and took hold of his feet and worshiped him (Mt 28:9). *Hail Mary ...*

6. On the evening of that day,... the doors being shut where the disciples were, for fear of the Jews, Jesus came and stood among them and said to them, "Peace be with you" (Jn 20:19). *Hail Mary ...*

7. When he had said this, he showed them his hands and his side (Jn 20:20). *Hail Mary ...*

8. [Jesus] said to Thomas, "Put your finger here, and see my hands; and put out your hand, and place it in my side; do not be faithless, but believing" (Jn 20:27). *Hail Mary ...*

9. Thomas answered him, "My Lord and my God!" (Jn 20:28). *Hail Mary ...*

10. Jesus said to him, "Have you believed because you have seen me? Blessed are those who have not seen and yet believe" (Jn 20:29). *Hail Mary ...*

The Second Glorious Mystery
The Ascension

1. To them [Jesus] presented himself alive after his passion by many proofs, appearing to them during forty days, and speaking of the kingdom of God (Acts 1:3). *Hail Mary ...*

2. So when they had come together, they asked him, "Lord, will you at this time restore the kingdom to Israel?" (Acts 1:6). *Hail Mary ...*

3. He said to them, "It is not for you to know times or seasons which the Father has fixed by his own authority" (Acts 1:7). *Hail Mary ...*

4. "But you shall receive power when the Holy Spirit has come upon you" (Acts 1:8). *Hail Mary ...*

5. "And you shall be my witnesses in Jerusalem and in all Judea and Samaria and to the end of the earth" (Acts 1:8). *Hail Mary ...*

6. And when he had said this, as they were looking on, he was lifted up, and a cloud took him out of their sight (Acts 1:9). *Hail Mary ...*

7. So then the Lord Jesus, after he had spoken to them, was taken up into heaven, and sat down at the right hand of God (Mk 16:19). *Hail Mary ...*

8. And while they were gazing into heaven as he went, behold, two men stood by them in white robes (Acts 1:10). *Hail Mary ...*

9. [The two men] said, "Men of Galilee, why do you stand looking into heaven?" (Acts 2:11). *Hail Mary ...*

10. "This Jesus, who was taken up from you into heaven, will come in the same way as you saw him go into heaven" (Acts 2:11). *Hail Mary ...*

The Third Glorious Mystery
The Descent of the Holy Spirit

1. When the day of Pentecost had come, they were all together in one place (Acts 2:1). *Hail Mary ...*

2. And suddenly a sound came from heaven like the rush of a mighty wind, and it filled all the house where they were sitting (Acts 2:2). *Hail Mary ...*

3. And there appeared to them tongues as of fire, distributed and resting on each one of them (Acts 2:3). *Hail Mary ...*

4. And they were all filled with the Holy Spirit and began to speak in other tongues, as the Spirit gave them utterance (Acts 2:4). *Hail Mary ...*

5. Now there were dwelling in Jerusalem Jews, devout men from every nation under heaven. And at this sound the multitude came together, and they were bewildered, because each one heard them speaking in his own language (Acts 2:5-6). *Hail Mary ...*

6. But Peter, standing with the eleven, lifted up his voice and addressed them, "Men of Judea and all who dwell in Jerusalem,... this is what was spoken by the prophet Joel" (Acts 2:14, 16). *Hail Mary ...*

7. "And in the last days it shall be, God declares, that I will pour out my Spirit upon all flesh, and your sons and your daughters shall prophesy" (Acts 2:17; see Joel 2:28). *Hail Mary ...*

8. "Let all the house of Israel therefore know assuredly that God has made him both Lord and Christ, this Jesus whom you crucified" (Acts 2:36). *Hail Mary ...*

9. And Peter said to them, "Repent, and be baptized every one of you in the name of Jesus Christ for the forgiveness of your sins; and you shall receive the gift of the Holy Spirit"(Acts 2:38). *Hail Mary ...*

10. So those who received his word were baptized, and there were added that day about three thousand souls (Acts 2:41). *Hail Mary ...*

The Fourth Glorious Mystery
The Assumption of Mary

1. "Arise, my love, my fair one, and come away" (Sg 2:10). *Hail Mary ...*

2. "You are all fair, my love; there is no flaw in you" (Sg 4:7). *Hail Mary ...*

3. Arise, O Lord, and go to thy resting place, thou and the ark of thy might (Ps 132:8). *Hail Mary ...*

4. Then God's temple in heaven was opened, and the ark of his covenant was seen within his temple (Rv 11:19). *Hail Mary ...*

5. And a great portent appeared in heaven, a woman clothed with the sun (Rv 12:1). *Hail Mary ...*

6. "Who is this that looks forth like the dawn, fair as the moon, bright as the sun?" (Sg 6:10). *Hail Mary ...*

7. "Hail, full of grace, the Lord is with you!" (Lk 1:28). *Hail Mary ...*

8. "Blessed are you among women" (Lk 1:42). *Hail Mary ...*

9. "For behold, henceforth all generations will call me blessed; for he who is mighty has done great things for me" (Lk 1:48-49). *Hail Mary ...*

10. "You are the exaltation of Jerusalem, you are the great glory of Israel, you are the great pride of our nation!" (Jdt 15:9). *Hail Mary ...*

The Fifth Glorious Mystery
The Crowning of Mary

1. So Bathsheba went to King Solomon,... and the king rose to meet her, and bowed down to her (1 Kgs 2:19). *Hail Mary ...*

2. Then he sat on his throne, and had a seat brought for the king's mother; and she sat on his right (1 Kgs 2:19). *Hail Mary ...*

3. Then she said, "I have one small request to make of you; do not refuse me" (1 Kgs 2:20). *Hail Mary ...*

4. And the king said to her, "Make your request, my mother; for I will not refuse you" (1 Kgs 2:20). *Hail Mary ...*

5. [The angel said to Mary,] "And behold, you will conceive in your womb and bear a son ... and the Lord God will give to him the throne of his father David" (Lk 1:31-32). *Hail Mary ...*

6. [Elizabeth said to Mary,] "And why is this granted me, that the mother of my Lord should come to me?" (Lk 1:43). *Hail Mary ...*

7. And a great portent appeared in heaven, a woman clothed with the sun, with the moon under her feet (Rv 12:1). *Hail Mary ...*

8. And on her head [was] a crown of twelve stars (Rv 12:1). *Hail Mary ...*

9. She brought forth a male child, one who is to rule all the nations with a rod of iron (Rv 12:5). *Hail Mary ...*

10. But her child was caught up to God and to his throne (Rv 12:5). *Hail Mary ...*

Appendix

APOSTOLIC LETTER ROSARIUM VIRGINIS MARIAE OF THE SUPREME PONTIFF JOHN PAUL II TO THE BISHOPS, CLERGY AND FAITHFUL ON THE MOST HOLY ROSARY

Introduction

1. The Rosary of the Virgin Mary, which gradually took form in the second millennium under the guidance of the Spirit of God, is a prayer loved by countless Saints and encouraged by the Magisterium. Simple yet profound, it still remains, at the dawn of this third millennium, a prayer of great significance, destined to bring forth a harvest of holiness. It blends easily into the spiritual journey of the Christian life, which, after two thousand years, has lost none of the freshness of its beginnings and feels drawn by the Spirit of God to "set out into the deep" *(duc in altum!)* in order once more to proclaim, and even cry out, before the world that Jesus Christ is Lord and Savior, "the way, and the truth and the life" (Jn 14:6), "the goal of human history and the point on which the desires of history and civilization turn".[1] The Rosary, though clearly Marian in character, is at heart a Christocentric prayer. In the sobriety of its elements, it has all the depth of the Gospel message in its entirety, of which it can be said to be a compendium.[2] It is an echo of the prayer of Mary, her perennial Magnificat for the work of the redemptive Incarnation which began in her virginal womb. With the Rosary, the Christian people sit at the school of Mary

and are led to contemplate the beauty on the face of Christ and to experience the depths of his love. Through the Rosary the faithful receive abundant grace, as though from the very hands of the Mother of the Redeemer.

The Popes and the Rosary

2. Numerous predecessors of mine attributed great importance to this prayer. Worthy of special note in this regard is Pope Leo XIII who on 1 September 1883 promulgated the Encyclical *Supremi Apostolatus Officio*,[3] a document of great worth, the first of his many statements about this prayer, in which he proposed the Rosary as an effective spiritual weapon against the evils afflicting society. Among the more recent Popes who, from the time of the Second Vatican Council, have distinguished themselves in promoting the Rosary I would mention Blessed John XXIII[4] and above all Pope Paul VI, who in his Apostolic Exhortation *Marialis Cultus* emphasized, in the spirit of the Second Vatican Council, the Rosary's evangelical character and its Christocentric inspiration. I myself have often encouraged the frequent recitation of the Rosary. From my youthful years this prayer has held an important place in my spiritual life. I was powerfully reminded of this during my recent visit to Poland, and in particular at the Shrine of Kalwaria. The Rosary has accompanied me in moments of joy and in moments of difficulty. To it I have entrusted any number of concerns; in it I have always found comfort. Twenty-four years ago, on 29 October 1978, scarcely two weeks after my election to the See of Peter, I frankly admitted: "The Rosary is my favorite prayer. A marvelous prayer! Marvelous in its simplicity and its depth. [...] It can be said that the Rosary is, in some sense, a prayer-commentary on the final chapter of the Vatican II Constitution *Lumen Gentium,* a chapter which discusses the wondrous presence of the Mother of God in the mystery

of Christ and the Church. Against the background of the words Ave Maria the principal events of the life of Jesus Christ pass before the eyes of the soul. They take shape in the complete series of the joyful, sorrowful and glorious mysteries, and they put us in living communion with Jesus through—we might say—the heart of his Mother. At the same time our heart can embrace in the decades of the Rosary all the events that make up the lives of individuals, families, nations, the Church, and all mankind. Our personal concerns and those of our neighbor, especially those who are closest to us, who are dearest to us. Thus the simple prayer of the Rosary marks the rhythm of human life".[5] With these words, dear brothers and sisters, I set the first year of my Pontificate within the daily rhythm of the Rosary. Today, as I begin the twenty-fifth year of my service as the Successor of Peter, I wish to do the same. How many graces have I received in these years from the Blessed Virgin through the Rosary: *Magnificat anima mea Dominum!* I wish to lift up my thanks to the Lord in the words of his Most Holy Mother, under whose protection I have placed my Petrine ministry: *Totus Tuus!*

October 2002—October 2003: The Year of the Rosary

3. Therefore, in continuity with my reflection in the Apostolic Letter *Novo Millennio Ineunte,* in which, after the experience of the Jubilee, I invited the people of God to "start afresh from Christ",[6] I have felt drawn to offer a reflection on the Rosary, as a kind of Marian complement to that Letter and an exhortation to contemplate the face of Christ in union with, and at the school of, his Most Holy Mother. To recite the Rosary is nothing other than to contemplate with Mary the face of Christ. As a way of highlighting this invitation, prompted by the forthcoming 120th anniversary of the aforementioned Encyclical of Leo XIII, I desire that during the course of this year the Rosary

should be especially emphasized and promoted in the various Christian communities. I therefore proclaim the year from October 2002 to October 2003 the Year of the Rosary. I leave this pastoral proposal to the initiative of each ecclesial community. It is not my intention to encumber but rather to complete and consolidate pastoral programmes of the Particular Churches. I am confident that the proposal will find a ready and generous reception. The Rosary, reclaimed in its full meaning, goes to the very heart of Christian life; it offers a familiar yet fruitful spiritual and educational opportunity for personal contemplation, the formation of the People of God, and the new evangelization. I am pleased to reaffirm this also in the joyful remembrance of another anniversary: the fortieth anniversary of the opening of the Second Vatican Ecumenical Council on October 11, 1962, the "great grace" disposed by the Spirit of God for the Church in our time.[7]

Objections to the Rosary

4. The timeliness of this proposal is evident from a number of considerations. First, the urgent need to counter a certain crisis of the Rosary, which in the present historical and theological context can risk being wrongly devalued, and therefore no longer taught to the younger generation. There are some who think that the centrality of the Liturgy, rightly stressed by the Second Vatican Ecumenical Council, necessarily entails giving lesser importance to the Rosary. Yet, as Pope Paul VI made clear, not only does this prayer not conflict with the Liturgy, it sustains it, since it serves as an excellent introduction and a faithful echo of the Liturgy, enabling people to participate fully and interiorly in it and to reap its fruits in their daily lives. Perhaps too, there are some who fear that the Rosary is somehow unecumenical because of its distinctly Marian character. Yet the Rosary clearly belongs to the kind of veneration of the Mother of God described by the Council: a

devotion directed to the Christological centre of the Christian faith, in such a way that "when the Mother is honored, the Son ... is duly known, loved and glorified".[8] If properly revitalized, the Rosary is an aid and certainly not a hindrance to ecumenism!

A path of contemplation

5. But the most important reason for strongly encouraging the practice of the Rosary is that it represents a most effective means of fostering among the faithful that commitment to the contemplation of the Christian mystery which I have proposed in the Apostolic Letter *Novo Millennio Ineunte* as a genuine "training in holiness": "What is needed is a Christian life distinguished above all in the art of prayer".[9] Inasmuch as contemporary culture, even amid so many indications to the contrary, has witnessed the flowering of a new call for spirituality, due also to the influence of other religions, it is more urgent than ever that our Christian communities should become "genuine schools of prayer".[10] The Rosary belongs among the finest and most praiseworthy traditions of Christian contemplation. Developed in the West, it is a typically meditative prayer, corresponding in some way to the "prayer of the heart" or "Jesus prayer" which took root in the soil of the Christian East.

Prayer for peace and for the family

6. A number of historical circumstances also make a revival of the Rosary quite timely. First of all, the need to implore from God the gift of peace. The Rosary has many times been proposed by my predecessors and myself as a prayer for peace. At the start of a millennium which began with the terrifying attacks of 11 September 2001, a millennium which witnesses every day in numerous parts of the world fresh scenes of bloodshed and violence, to rediscover the Rosary means

to immerse oneself in contemplation of the mystery of Christ who "is our peace", since he made "the two of us one, and broke down the dividing wall of hostility" (Eph 2:14). Consequently, one cannot recite the Rosary without feeling caught up in a clear commitment to advancing peace, especially in the land of Jesus, still so sorely afflicted and so close to the heart of every Christian. A similar need for commitment and prayer arises in relation to another critical contemporary issue: the family, the primary cell of society, increasingly menaced by forces of disintegration on both the ideological and practical planes, so as to make us fear for the future of this fundamental and indispensable institution and, with it, for the future of society as a whole. The revival of the Rosary in Christian families, within the context of a broader pastoral ministry to the family, will be an effective aid to countering the devastating effects of this crisis typical of our age.

"Behold, your Mother!" (Jn 19:27)

7. Many signs indicate that still today the Blessed Virgin desires to exercise through this same prayer that maternal concern to which the dying Redeemer entrusted, in the person of the beloved disciple, all the sons and daughters of the Church: "Woman, behold your son!" (Jn 19:26). Well-known are the occasions in the nineteenth and the twentieth centuries on which the Mother of Christ made her presence felt and her voice heard, in order to exhort the People of God to this form of contemplative prayer. I would mention in particular, on account of their great influence on the lives of Christians and the authoritative recognition they have received from the Church, the apparitions of Lourdes and of Fatima;[11] these shrines continue to be visited by great numbers of pilgrims seeking comfort and hope.

Following the witnesses

8. It would be impossible to name all the many Saints who discovered in the Rosary a genuine path to growth in holiness. We need but mention Saint Louis Marie Grignion de Montfort, the author of an excellent work on the Rosary,[12] and, closer to ourselves, Padre Pio of Pietrelcina, whom I recently had the joy of canonizing. As a true apostle of the Rosary, Blessed Bartolo Longo had a special charism. His path to holiness rested on an inspiration heard in the depths of his heart: "Whoever spreads the Rosary is saved!".[13] As a result, he felt called to build a Church dedicated to Our Lady of the Holy Rosary in Pompei, against the background of the ruins of the ancient city, which scarcely heard the proclamation of Christ before being buried in A.D. 79 during an eruption of Mount Vesuvius, only to emerge centuries later from its ashes as a witness to the lights and shadows of classical civilization. By his whole life's work and especially by the practice of the "Fifteen Saturdays", Bartolo Longo promoted the Christocentric and contemplative heart of the Rosary, and received great encouragement and support from Leo XIII, the "Pope of the Rosary".

CHAPTER I
CONTEMPLATING CHRIST WITH MARY

A face radiant as the sun

9. "And he was transfigured before them, and his face shone like the sun" (Mt 17:2). The Gospel scene of Christ's transfiguration, in which the three Apostles Peter, James and John appear entranced by the beauty of the Redeemer, can be seen as an icon of Christian contemplation. To look upon the face of Christ, to recognize its mystery amid the daily events and the sufferings of his human life, and then to grasp the divine splendour definitively revealed in the Risen Lord, seated in

glory at the right hand of the Father: this is the task of every follower of Christ and therefore the task of each one of us. In contemplating Christ's face we become open to receiving the mystery of Trinitarian life, experiencing ever anew the love of the Father and delighting in the joy of the Holy Spirit. Saint Paul's words can then be applied to us: "Beholding the glory of the Lord, we are being changed into his likeness, from one degree of glory to another; for this comes from the Lord who is the Spirit" (2 Cor 3:18).

Mary, model of contemplation

10. The contemplation of Christ has an incomparable model in Mary. In a unique way the face of the Son belongs to Mary. It was in her womb that Christ was formed, receiving from her a human resemblance which points to an even greater spiritual closeness. No one has ever devoted himself to the contemplation of the face of Christ as faithfully as Mary. The eyes of her heart already turned to him at the Annunciation, when she conceived him by the power of the Holy Spirit. In the months that followed she began to sense his presence and to picture his features. When at last she gave birth to him in Bethlehem, her eyes were able to gaze tenderly on the face of her Son, as she "wrapped him in swaddling cloths, and laid him in a manger" (Lk 2:7). Thereafter Mary's gaze, ever filled with adoration and wonder, would never leave him. At times it would be a questioning look, as in the episode of the finding in the Temple: "Son, why have you treated us so?" (Lk 2:48); it would always be a penetrating gaze, one capable of deeply understanding Jesus, even to the point of perceiving his hidden feelings and anticipating his decisions, as at Cana (cf. Jn 2:5). At other times it would be a look of sorrow, especially beneath the Cross, where her vision would still be that of a mother giving birth, for Mary not only shared the passion and death of her Son, she also

received the new son given to her in the beloved disciple (cf. Jn 19:26-27). On the morning of Easter hers would be a gaze radiant with the joy of the Resurrection, and finally, on the day of Pentecost, a gaze afire with the outpouring of the Spirit (cf. Acts 1:14).

Mary's memories

11. Mary lived with her eyes fixed on Christ, treasuring his every word: "She kept all these things, pondering them in her heart" (Lk 2:19; cf. 2:51). The memories of Jesus, impressed upon her heart, were always with her, leading her to reflect on the various moments of her life at her Son's side. In a way those memories were to be the "rosary" which she recited uninterruptedly throughout her earthly life. Even now, amid the joyful songs of the heavenly Jerusalem, the reasons for her thanksgiving and praise remain unchanged. They inspire her maternal concern for the pilgrim Church, in which she continues to relate her personal account of the Gospel. Mary constantly sets before the faithful the "mysteries" of her Son, with the desire that the contemplation of those mysteries will release all their saving power. In the recitation of the Rosary, the Christian community enters into contact with the memories and the contemplative gaze of Mary.

The Rosary, a contemplative prayer

12. The Rosary, precisely because it starts with Mary's own experience, is an exquisitely contemplative prayer. Without this contemplative dimension, it would lose its meaning, as Pope Paul VI clearly pointed out: "Without contemplation, the Rosary is a body without a soul, and its recitation runs the risk of becoming a mechanical repetition of formulas, in violation of the admonition of Christ: 'In praying do not heap up empty phrases as the Gentiles do; for they think they will be heard for their many words' (Mt 6:7). By its nature the recitation of

the Rosary calls for a quiet rhythm and a lingering pace, helping the individual to meditate on the mysteries of the Lord's life as seen through the eyes of her who was closest to the Lord. In this way the unfathomable riches of these mysteries are disclosed".[14] It is worth pausing to consider this profound insight of Paul VI, in order to bring out certain aspects of the Rosary which show that it is really a form of Christocentric contemplation.

Remembering Christ with Mary

13. Mary's contemplation is above all a remembering. We need to understand this word in the biblical sense of remembrance *(zakar)* as a making present of the works brought about by God in the history of salvation. The Bible is an account of saving events culminating in Christ himself. These events not only belong to "yesterday"; they are also part of the "today" of salvation. This making present comes about above all in the Liturgy: what God accomplished centuries ago did not only affect the direct witnesses of those events; it continues to affect people in every age with its gift of grace. To some extent this is also true of every other devout approach to those events: to "remember" them in a spirit of faith and love is to be open to the grace which Christ won for us by the mysteries of his life, death and resurrection. Consequently, while it must be reaffirmed with the Second Vatican Council that the Liturgy, as the exercise of the priestly office of Christ and an act of public worship, is "the summit to which the activity of the Church is directed and the font from which all its power flows",[15] it is also necessary to recall that the spiritual life "is not limited solely to participation in the liturgy. Christians, while they are called to prayer in common, must also go to their own rooms to pray to their Father in secret (cf. Mt 6:6); indeed, according to the teaching of the Apostle, they must pray without ceasing (cf. 1 Thes 5:17)".[16]

The Rosary, in its own particular way, is part of this varied panorama of "ceaseless" prayer. If the Liturgy, as the activity of Christ and the Church, is a saving action par excellence, the Rosary too, as a "meditation" with Mary on Christ, is a salutary contemplation. By immersing us in the mysteries of the Redeemer's life, it ensures that what he has done and what the liturgy makes present is profoundly assimilated and shapes our existence.

Learning Christ from Mary

14. Christ is the supreme Teacher, the revealer and the one revealed. It is not just a question of learning what he taught but of "learning him". In this regard could we have any better teacher than Mary? From the divine standpoint, the Spirit is the interior teacher who leads us to the full truth of Christ (cf. Jn 14:26; 15:26; 16:13). But among creatures no one knows Christ better than Mary; no one can introduce us to a profound knowledge of his mystery better than his Mother. The first of the "signs" worked by Jesus—the changing of water into wine at the marriage in Cana—clearly presents Mary in the guise of a teacher, as she urges the servants to do what Jesus commands (cf. Jn 2:5). We can imagine that she would have done likewise for the disciples after Jesus' Ascension, when she joined them in awaiting the Holy Spirit and supported them in their first mission. Contemplating the scenes of the Rosary in union with Mary is a means of learning from her to "read" Christ, to discover his secrets and to understand his message. This school of Mary is all the more effective if we consider that she teaches by obtaining for us in abundance the gifts of the Holy Spirit, even as she offers us the incomparable example of her own "pilgrimage of faith".[17] As we contemplate each mystery of her Son's life, she invites us to do as she did at the Annunciation: to ask humbly the questions which open us to the light, in order to end with the obedience of faith:

"Behold I am the handmaid of the Lord; be it done to me according to your word" (Lk 1:38).

Being conformed to Christ with Mary

15. Christian spirituality is distinguished by the disciple's commitment to become conformed ever more fully to his Master (cf. Rom 8:29; Phil 3:10, 12). The outpouring of the Holy Spirit in Baptism grafts the believer like a branch onto the vine which is Christ (cf. Jn 15:5) and makes him a member of Christ's mystical Body (cf. 1 Cor 12:12; Rom 12:5). This initial unity, however, calls for a growing assimilation which will increasingly shape the conduct of the disciple in accordance with the "mind" of Christ: "Have this mind among yourselves, which was in Christ Jesus" (Phil 2:5). In the words of the Apostle, we are called "to put on the Lord Jesus Christ" (cf. Rom 13:14; Gal 3:27). In the spiritual journey of the Rosary, based on the constant contemplation—in Mary's company—of the face of Christ, this demanding ideal of being conformed to him is pursued through an association which could be described in terms of friendship. We are thereby enabled to enter naturally into Christ's life and as it were to share his deepest feelings. In this regard Blessed Bartolo Longo has written: "Just as two friends, frequently in each other's company, tend to develop similar habits, so too, by holding familiar converse with Jesus and the Blessed Virgin, by meditating on the mysteries of the Rosary and by living the same life in Holy Communion, we can become, to the extent of our lowliness, similar to them and can learn from these supreme models a life of humility, poverty, hiddenness, patience and perfection".[18] In this process of being conformed to Christ in the Rosary, we entrust ourselves in a special way to the maternal care of the Blessed Virgin. She who is both the Mother of Christ and a member of the Church, indeed her "pre-eminent and altogether singular member",[19] is at

the same time the "Mother of the Church". As such, she continually brings to birth children for the mystical Body of her Son. She does so through her intercession, imploring upon them the inexhaustible out-pouring of the Spirit. Mary is the perfect icon of the motherhood of the Church. The Rosary mystically transports us to Mary's side as she is busy watching over the human growth of Christ in the home of Nazareth. This enables her to train us and to mold us with the same care, until Christ is "fully formed" in us (cf. Gal 4:19). This role of Mary, totally grounded in that of Christ and radically subordinated to it, "in no way obscures or diminishes the unique mediation of Christ, but rather shows its power".[20] This is the luminous principle expressed by the Second Vatican Council which I have so powerfully experienced in my own life and have made the basis of my episcopal motto: *Totus Tuus*.[21] The motto is of course inspired by the teaching of Saint Louis Marie Grignion de Montfort, who explained in the following words Mary's role in the process of our configuration to Christ: "Our entire perfection consists in being conformed, united and consecrated to Jesus Christ. Hence the most perfect of all devotions is undoubtedly that which conforms, unites and consecrates us most perfectly to Jesus Christ. Now, since Mary is of all creatures the one most conformed to Jesus Christ, it follows that among all devotions that which most consecrates and conforms a soul to our Lord is devotion to Mary, his Holy Mother, and that the more a soul is consecrated to her the more will it be consecrated to Jesus Christ".[22] Never as in the Rosary do the life of Jesus and that of Mary appear so deeply joined. Mary lives only in Christ and for Christ!

Praying to Christ with Mary
16. Jesus invited us to turn to God with insistence and the confidence that we will be heard: "Ask, and it will be given to you; seek, and you

will find; knock, and it will be opened to you" (Mt 7:7). The basis for this power of prayer is the goodness of the Father, but also the mediation of Christ himself (cf. 1 Jn 2:1) and the working of the Holy Spirit who "intercedes for us" according to the will of God (cf. Rom 8:26-27). For "we do not know how to pray as we ought" (Rom 8:26), and at times we are not heard "because we ask wrongly" (cf. Jas 4:2-3). In support of the prayer which Christ and the Spirit cause to rise in our hearts, Mary intervenes with her maternal intercession. "The prayer of the Church is sustained by the prayer of Mary".[23] If Jesus, the one Mediator, is the Way of our prayer, then Mary, his purest and most transparent reflection, shows us the Way. "Beginning with Mary's unique cooperation with the working of the Holy Spirit, the Churches developed their prayer to the Holy Mother of God, centering it on the person of Christ manifested in his mysteries".[24] At the wedding of Cana the Gospel clearly shows the power of Mary's intercession as she makes known to Jesus the needs of others: "They have no wine" (Jn 2:3). The Rosary is both meditation and supplication. Insistent prayer to the Mother of God is based on confidence that her maternal intercession can obtain all things from the heart of her Son. She is "all-powerful by grace", to use the bold expression, which needs to be properly understood, of Blessed Bartolo Longo in his *Supplication to Our Lady*.[25] This is a conviction which, beginning with the Gospel, has grown ever more firm in the experience of the Christian people. The supreme poet Dante expresses it marvellously in the lines sung by Saint Bernard: "Lady, thou art so great and so powerful, that whoever desires grace yet does not turn to thee, would have his desire fly without wings".[26] When in the Rosary we plead with Mary, the sanctuary of the Holy Spirit (cf. Lk 1:35), she intercedes for us before the Father who filled her with grace and before the Son born of her womb, praying with us and for us.

Proclaiming Christ with Mary

17. The Rosary is also a path of proclamation and increasing knowledge, in which the mystery of Christ is presented again and again at different levels of the Christian experience. Its form is that of a prayerful and contemplative presentation, capable of forming Christians according to the heart of Christ. When the recitation of the Rosary combines all the elements needed for an effective meditation, especially in its communal celebration in parishes and shrines, it can present a significant catechetical opportunity which pastors should use to advantage. In this way too Our Lady of the Rosary continues her work of proclaiming Christ. The history of the Rosary shows how this prayer was used in particular by the Dominicans at a difficult time for the Church due to the spread of heresy. Today we are facing new challenges. Why should we not once more have recourse to the Rosary, with the same faith as those who have gone before us? The Rosary retains all its power and continues to be a valuable pastoral resource for every good evangelizer.

CHAPTER II
MYSTERIES OF CHRIST—MYSTERIES OF HIS MOTHER

The Rosary, "a compendium of the Gospel"

18. The only way to approach the contemplation of Christ's face is by listening in the Spirit to the Father's voice, since "no one knows the Son except the Father" (Mt 11:27). In the region of Caesarea Philippi, Jesus responded to Peter's confession of faith by indicating the source of that clear intuition of his identity: "Flesh and blood has not revealed this to you, but my Father who is in heaven" (Mt 16:17). What is needed, then, is a revelation from above. In order to receive that revelation, attentive listening is indispensable: "Only the experience of

silence and prayer offers the proper setting for the growth and development of a true, faithful and consistent knowledge of that mystery".[27] The Rosary is one of the traditional paths of Christian
prayer directed to the contemplation of Christ's face. Pope Paul VI
described it in these words: "As a Gospel prayer, centered on the mystery
of the redemptive Incarnation, the Rosary is a prayer with a clearly
Christological orientation. Its most characteristic element, in fact, the
litany-like succession of Hail Marys, becomes in itself an unceasing
praise of Christ, who is the ultimate object both of the Angel's
announcement and of the greeting of the Mother of John the Baptist:
'Blessed is the fruit of your womb' (Lk 1:42). We would go further and
say that the succession of Hail Marys constitutes the warp on which is
woven the contemplation of the mysteries. The Jesus that each Hail
Mary recalls is the same Jesus whom the succession of mysteries proposes to us now as the Son of God, now as the Son of the Virgin".[28]

A proposed addition to the traditional pattern
19. Of the many mysteries of Christ's life, only a few are indicated by
the Rosary in the form that has become generally established with the
seal of the Church's approval. The selection was determined by the origin of the prayer, which was based on the number 150, the number of
the psalms in the psalter. I believe, however, that to bring out fully the
Christological depth of the Rosary it would be suitable to make an
addition to the traditional pattern which, while left to the freedom of
individuals and communities, could broaden it to include the mysteries of Christ's public ministry between his Baptism and his Passion. In
the course of those mysteries we contemplate important aspects of the
person of Christ as the definitive revelation of God. Declared the
beloved Son of the Father at the Baptism in the Jordan, Christ is the
one who announces the coming of the Kingdom, bears witness to it in

his works and proclaims its demands. It is during the years of his public ministry that the mystery of Christ is most evidently a mystery of light: "While I am in the world, I am the light of the world" (Jn 9:5). Consequently, for the Rosary to become more fully a "compendium of the Gospel", it is fitting to add, following reflection on the Incarnation and the hidden life of Christ (the joyful mysteries) and before focusing on the sufferings of his Passion (the sorrowful mysteries) and the triumph of his Resurrection (the glorious mysteries), a meditation on certain particularly significant moments in his public ministry (the mysteries of light). This addition of these new mysteries, without prejudice to any essential aspect of the prayer's traditional format, is meant to give it fresh life and to enkindle renewed interest in the Rosary's place within Christian spirituality as a true doorway to the depths of the Heart of Christ, ocean of joy and of light, of suffering and of glory.

The Joyful Mysteries

20. The first five decades, the "joyful mysteries", are marked by the joy radiating from the event of the Incarnation. This is clear from the very first mystery, the Annunciation, where Gabriel's greeting to the Virgin of Nazareth is linked to an invitation to messianic joy: "Rejoice, Mary". The whole of salvation history, in some sense the entire history of the world, has led up to this greeting. If it is the Father's plan to unite all things in Christ (cf. Eph 1:10), then the whole of the universe is in some way touched by the divine favor with which the Father looks upon Mary and makes her the Mother of his Son. The whole of humanity, in turn, is embraced by the *fiat* with which she readily agrees to the will of God. Exultation is the keynote of the encounter with Elizabeth, where the sound of Mary's voice and the presence of Christ in her womb cause John to "leap for joy" (cf. Lk 1:44). Gladness also fills the scene in Bethlehem, when the birth of the divine Child,

the Savior of the world, is announced by the song of the angels and proclaimed to the shepherds as "news of great joy" (Lk 2:10). The final two mysteries, while preserving this climate of joy, already point to the drama yet to come. The Presentation in the Temple not only expresses the joy of the Child's consecration and the ecstasy of the aged Simeon; it also records the prophecy that Christ will be a "sign of contradiction" for Israel and that a sword will pierce his mother's heart (cf Lk 2:34-35). Joy mixed with drama marks the fifth mystery, the finding of the twelve-year-old Jesus in the Temple. Here he appears in his divine wisdom as he listens and raises questions, already in effect one who "teaches". The revelation of his mystery as the Son wholly dedicated to his Father's affairs proclaims the radical nature of the Gospel, in which even the closest of human relationships are challenged by the absolute demands of the Kingdom. Mary and Joseph, fearful and anxious, "did not understand" his words (Lk 2:50). To meditate upon the "joyful" mysteries, then, is to enter into the ultimate causes and the deepest meaning of Christian joy. It is to focus on the realism of the mystery of the Incarnation and on the obscure foreshadowing of the mystery of the saving Passion. Mary leads us to discover the secret of Christian joy, reminding us that Christianity is, first and foremost, *evangelion,* "good news", which has as its heart and its whole content the person of Jesus Christ, the Word made flesh, the one Savior of the world.

The Mysteries of Light

21. Moving on from the infancy and the hidden life in Nazareth to the public life of Jesus, our contemplation brings us to those mysteries which may be called in a special way "mysteries of light". Certainly the whole mystery of Christ is a mystery of light. He is the "light of the world" (Jn 8:12). Yet this truth emerges in a special way during the years of his public life, when he proclaims the Gospel of the Kingdom.

In proposing to the Christian community five significant moments—
"luminous" mysteries—during this phase of Christ's life, I think that
the following can be fittingly singled out: (1) his Baptism in the
Jordan, (2) his self-manifestation at the wedding of Cana, (3) his
proclamation of the Kingdom of God, with his call to conversion, (4)
his Transfiguration, and finally, (5) his institution of the Eucharist, as
the sacramental expression of the Paschal Mystery. Each of these mysteries is a revelation of the Kingdom now present in the very person of
Jesus. The Baptism in the Jordan is first of all a mystery of light. Here,
as Christ descends into the waters, the innocent one who became "sin"
for our sake (cf. 2 Cor 5:21), the heavens open wide and the voice of
the Father declares him the beloved Son (cf. Mt 3:17 and parallels),
while the Spirit descends on him to invest him with the mission which
he is to carry out. Another mystery of light is the first of the signs,
given at Cana (cf. Jn 2:1-12), when Christ changes water into wine
and opens the hearts of the disciples to faith, thanks to the intervention of Mary, the first among believers. Another mystery of light is the
preaching by which Jesus proclaims the coming of the Kingdom of
God, calls to conversion (cf. Mk 1:15) and forgives the sins of all who
draw near to him in humble trust (cf. Mk 2:3-12; Lk 7:47-48): the
inauguration of that ministry of mercy which he continues to exercise
until the end of the world, particularly through the Sacrament of
Reconciliation which he has entrusted to his Church (cf. Jn 20:22-23).
The mystery of light par excellence is the Transfiguration, traditionally
believed to have taken place on Mount Tabor. The glory of the
Godhead shines forth from the face of Christ as the Father commands
the astonished Apostles to "listen to him" (cf. Lk 9:35 and parallels)
and to prepare to experience with him the agony of the Passion, so as
to come with him to the joy of the Resurrection and a life transfigured
by the Holy Spirit. A final mystery of light is the institution of the

Eucharist, in which Christ offers his body and blood as food under the signs of bread and wine, and testifies "to the end" his love for humanity (Jn 13:1), for whose salvation he will offer himself in sacrifice. In these mysteries, apart from the miracle at Cana, the presence of Mary remains in the background. The Gospels make only the briefest reference to her occasional presence at one moment or other during the preaching of Jesus (cf. Mk 3:31-5; Jn 2:12), and they give no indication that she was present at the Last Supper and the institution of the Eucharist. Yet the role she assumed at Cana in some way accompanies Christ throughout his ministry. The revelation made directly by the Father at the Baptism in the Jordan and echoed by John the Baptist is placed upon Mary's lips at Cana, and it becomes the great maternal counsel which Mary addresses to the Church of every age: "Do whatever he tells you" (Jn 2:5). This counsel is a fitting introduction to the words and signs of Christ's public ministry and it forms the Marian foundation of all the "mysteries of light".

The Sorrowful Mysteries

22. The Gospels give great prominence to the sorrowful mysteries of Christ. From the beginning Christian piety, especially during the Lenten devotion of the *Way of the Cross,* has focused on the individual moments of the Passion, realizing that here is found the culmination of the revelation of God's love and the source of our salvation. The Rosary selects certain moments from the Passion, inviting the faithful to contemplate them in their hearts and to relive them. The sequence of meditations begins with Gethsemane, where Christ experiences a moment of great anguish before the will of the Father, against which the weakness of the flesh would be tempted to rebel. There Jesus encounters all the temptations and confronts all the sins of humanity, in order to say to the Father: "Not my will but yours be done" (Lk 22:42

and parallels). This "Yes" of Christ reverses the "No" of our first parents in the Garden of Eden. And the cost of this faithfulness to the Father's will is made clear in the following mysteries; by his scourging, his crowning with thorns, his carrying the Cross and his death on the Cross, the Lord is cast into the most abject suffering: *Ecce homo!* This abject suffering reveals not only the love of God but also the meaning of man himself. Ecce homo: the meaning, origin and fulfilment of man is to be found in Christ, the God who humbles himself out of love "even unto death, death on a cross" (Phil 2:8). The sorrowful mysteries help the believer to relive the death of Jesus, to stand at the foot of the Cross beside Mary, to enter with her into the depths of God's love for man and to experience all its life-giving power.

The Glorious Mysteries

23. "The contemplation of Christ's face cannot stop at the image of the Crucified One. He is the Risen One!"[29] The Rosary has always expressed this knowledge born of faith and invited the believer to pass beyond the darkness of the Passion in order to gaze upon Christ's glory in the Resurrection and Ascension. Contemplating the Risen One, Christians rediscover the reasons for their own faith (cf. 1 Cor 15:14) and relive the joy not only of those to whom Christ appeared—the Apostles, Mary Magdalene and the disciples on the road to Emmaus—but also the joy of Mary, who must have had an equally intense experience of the new life of her glorified Son. In the Ascension, Christ was raised in glory to the right hand of the Father, while Mary herself would be raised to that same glory in the Assumption, enjoying beforehand, by a unique privilege, the destiny reserved for all the just at the resurrection of the dead. Crowned in glory—as she appears in the last glorious mystery—Mary shines forth as Queen of the Angels and Saints, the anticipation and the supreme

realization of the eschatological state of the Church. At the center of this unfolding sequence of the glory of the Son and the Mother, the Rosary sets before us the third glorious mystery, Pentecost, which reveals the face of the Church as a family gathered together with Mary, enlivened by the powerful outpouring of the Spirit and ready for the mission of evangelization. The contemplation of this scene, like that of the other glorious mysteries, ought to lead the faithful to an ever greater appreciation of their new life in Christ, lived in the heart of the Church, a life of which the scene of Pentecost itself is the great "icon". The glorious mysteries thus lead the faithful to greater hope for the eschatological goal towards which they journey as members of the pilgrim People of God in history. This can only impel them to bear courageous witness to that "good news" which gives meaning to their entire existence.

From "mysteries" to the "Mystery": Mary's way

24. The cycles of meditation proposed by the Holy Rosary are by no means exhaustive, but they do bring to mind what is essential and they awaken in the soul a thirst for a knowledge of Christ continually nourished by the pure source of the Gospel. Every individual event in the life of Christ, as narrated by the Evangelists, is resplendent with the Mystery that surpasses all understanding (cf. Eph 3:19): the Mystery of the Word made flesh, in whom "all the fullness of God dwells bodily" (Col 2:9). For this reason the *Catechism of the Catholic Church* places great emphasis on the mysteries of Christ, pointing out that "everything in the life of Jesus is a sign of his Mystery".[30] The *"duc in altum"* of the Church of the third millennium will be determined by the ability of Christians to enter into the "perfect knowledge of God's mystery, of Christ, in whom are hidden all the treasures of wisdom and knowledge" (Col 2:2-3). The Letter to the Ephesians makes

this heartfelt prayer for all the baptized: "May Christ dwell in your hearts through faith, so that you, being rooted and grounded in love, may have power ... to know the love of Christ which surpasses knowledge, that you may be filled with all the fullness of God" (3:17-19).

The Rosary is at the service of this ideal; it offers the "secret" which leads easily to a profound and inward knowledge of Christ. We might call it Mary's way. It is the way of the example of the Virgin of Nazareth, a woman of faith, of silence, of attentive listening. It is also the way of a Marian devotion inspired by knowledge of the inseparable bond between Christ and his Blessed Mother: the mysteries of Christ are also in some sense the mysteries of his Mother, even when they do not involve her directly, for she lives from him and through him. By making our own the words of the Angel Gabriel and Saint Elizabeth contained in the Hail Mary, we find ourselves constantly drawn to seek out afresh in Mary, in her arms and in her heart, the "blessed fruit of her womb" (cf Lk 1:42).

Mystery of Christ, mystery of man

25. In my testimony of 1978 mentioned above, where I described the Rosary as my favourite prayer, I used an idea to which I would like to return. I said then that "the simple prayer of the Rosary marks the rhythm of human life".[31] In the light of what has been said so far on the mysteries of Christ, it is not difficult to go deeper into this anthropological significance of the Rosary, which is far deeper than may appear at first sight. Anyone who contemplates Christ through the various stages of his life cannot fail to perceive in him the truth about man. This is the great affirmation of the Second Vatican Council which I have so often discussed in my own teaching since the Encyclical Letter *Redemptor Hominis:* "It is only in the mystery of the Word made flesh that the mystery of man is seen in its true light".[32]

The Rosary helps to open up the way to this light. Following in the path of Christ, in whom man's path is "recapitulated",[33] revealed and redeemed, believers come face to face with the image of the true man. Contemplating Christ's birth, they learn of the sanctity of life; seeing the household of Nazareth, they learn the original truth of the family according to God's plan; listening to the Master in the mysteries of his public ministry, they find the light which leads them to enter the Kingdom of God; and following him on the way to Calvary, they learn the meaning of salvific suffering. Finally, contemplating Christ and his Blessed Mother in glory, they see the goal towards which each of us is called, if we allow ourselves to be healed and transformed by the Holy Spirit. It could be said that each mystery of the Rosary, carefully meditated, sheds light on the mystery of man. At the same time, it becomes natural to bring to this encounter with the sacred humanity of the Redeemer all the problems, anxieties, labors and endeavours which go to make up our lives. "Cast your burden on the Lord and he will sustain you" (Ps 55:22). To pray the Rosary is to hand over our burdens to the merciful hearts of Christ and his Mother. Twenty-five years later, thinking back over the difficulties which have also been part of my exercise of the Petrine ministry, I feel the need to say once more, as a warm invitation to everyone to experience it personally: the Rosary does indeed "mark the rhythm of human life", bringing it into harmony with the "rhythm" of God's own life, in the joyful communion of the Holy Trinity, our life's destiny and deepest longing.

CHAPTER III
"FOR ME, TO LIVE IS CHRIST"

The Rosary, a way of assimilating the mystery

26. Meditation on the mysteries of Christ is proposed in the Rosary by means of a method designed to assist in their assimilation. It is a method based on repetition. This applies above all to the Hail Mary, repeated ten times in each mystery. If this repetition is considered superficially, there could be a temptation to see the Rosary as a dry and boring exercise. It is quite another thing, however, when the Rosary is thought of as an outpouring of that love which tirelessly returns to the person loved with expressions similar in their content but ever fresh in terms of the feeling pervading them. In Christ, God has truly assumed a "heart of flesh". Not only does God have a divine heart, rich in mercy and in forgiveness, but also a human heart, capable of all the stirrings of affection. If we needed evidence for this from the Gospel, we could easily find it in the touching dialogue between Christ and Peter after the Resurrection: "Simon, son of John, do you love me?" Three times this question is put to Peter, and three times he gives the reply: "Lord, you know that I love you" (cf. Jn 21:15-17). Over and above the specific meaning of this passage, so important for Peter's mission, none can fail to recognize the beauty of this triple repetition, in which the insistent request and the corresponding reply are expressed in terms familiar from the universal experience of human love. To understand the Rosary, one has to enter into the psychological dynamic proper to love. One thing is clear: although the repeated Hail Mary is addressed directly to Mary, it is to Jesus that the act of love is ultimately directed, with her and through her. The repetition is nourished by the desire to be conformed ever more completely to Christ, the true program of the Christian life. Saint Paul expressed this project with words of fire: "For

me to live is Christ and to die is gain" (Phil 1:21). And again: "It is no longer I that live, but Christ lives in me" (Gal 2:20). The Rosary helps us to be conformed ever more closely to Christ until we attain true holiness.

A valid method ...

27. We should not be surprised that our relationship with Christ makes use of a method. God communicates himself to us respecting our human nature and its vital rhythms. Hence, while Christian spirituality is familiar with the most sublime forms of mystical silence in which images, words and gestures are all, so to speak, superseded by an intense and ineffable union with God, it normally engages the whole person in all his complex psychological, physical and relational reality. This becomes apparent in the liturgy. Sacraments and sacramentals are structured as a series of rites which bring into play all the dimensions of the person. The same applies to non-liturgical prayer. This is confirmed by the fact that, in the East, the most characteristic prayer of Christological meditation, centered on the words "Lord Jesus Christ, Son of God, have mercy on me, a sinner"[34] is traditionally linked to the rhythm of breathing; while this practice favors perseverance in the prayer, it also in some way embodies the desire for Christ to become the breath, the soul and the "all" of one's life.

... which can nevertheless be improved.

28. I mentioned in my Apostolic Letter *Novo Millennio Ineunte* that the West is now experiencing a renewed demand for meditation, which at times leads to a keen interest in aspects of other religions.[35] Some Christians, limited in their knowledge of the Christian contemplative tradition, are attracted by those forms of prayer. While the latter contain many elements which are positive and at times compatible

with Christian experience, they are often based on ultimately unacceptable premises. Much in vogue among these approaches are methods aimed at attaining a high level of spiritual concentration by using techniques of a psychophysical, repetitive and symbolic nature. The Rosary is situated within this broad gamut of religious phenomena, but it is distinguished by characteristics of its own which correspond to specifically Christian requirements. In effect, the Rosary is simply a method of contemplation. As a method, it serves as a means to an end and cannot become an end in itself. All the same, as the fruit of centuries of experience, this method should not be undervalued. In its favor one could cite the experience of countless Saints. This is not to say, however, that the method cannot be improved. Such is the intent of the addition of the new series of *mysteria lucis* to the overall cycle of mysteries and of the few suggestions which I am proposing in this Letter regarding its manner of recitation. These suggestions, while respecting the well-established structure of this prayer, are intended to help the faithful to understand it in the richness of its symbolism and in harmony with the demands of daily life. Otherwise there is a risk that the Rosary would not only fail to produce the intended spiritual effects, but even that the beads, with which it is usually said, could come to be regarded as some kind of amulet or magic object, thereby radically distorting their meaning and function.

Announcing each mystery

29. Announcing each mystery, and perhaps even using a suitable icon to portray it, is as it were to open up a scenario on which to focus our attention. The words direct the imagination and the mind towards a particular episode or moment in the life of Christ. In the Church's traditional spirituality, the veneration of icons and the many devotions appealing to the senses, as well as the method of prayer proposed by

Saint Ignatius of Loyola in the Spiritual Exercises, make use of visual and imaginative elements (the *compositio loci*), judged to be of great help in concentrating the mind on the particular mystery. This is a methodology, moreover, which corresponds to the inner logic of the Incarnation: in Jesus, God wanted to take on human features. It is through his bodily reality that we are led into contact with the mystery of his divinity. This need for concreteness finds further expression in the announcement of the various mysteries of the Rosary. Obviously these mysteries neither replace the Gospel nor exhaust its content. The Rosary, therefore, is no substitute for *lectio divina;* on the contrary, it presupposes and promotes it. Yet, even though the mysteries contemplated in the Rosary, even with the addition of the *mysteria lucis,* do no more than outline the fundamental elements of the life of Christ, they easily draw the mind to a more expansive reflection on the rest of the Gospel, especially when the Rosary is prayed in a setting of prolonged recollection.

Listening to the word of God

30. In order to supply a Biblical foundation and greater depth to our meditation, it is helpful to follow the announcement of the mystery with the proclamation of a related Biblical passage, long or short, depending on the circumstances. No other words can ever match the efficacy of the inspired word. As we listen, we are certain that this is the word of God, spoken for today and spoken "for me". If received in this way, the word of God can become part of the Rosary's methodology of repetition without giving rise to the ennui derived from the simple recollection of something already well known. It is not a matter of recalling information but of allowing God to speak. In certain solemn communal celebrations, this word can be appropriately illustrated by a brief commentary.

Silence

31. Listening and meditation are nourished by silence. After the announcement of the mystery and the proclamation of the word, it is fitting to pause and focus one's attention for a suitable period of time on the mystery concerned, before moving into vocal prayer. A discovery of the importance of silence is one of the secrets of practicing contemplation and meditation. One drawback of a society dominated by technology and the mass media is the fact that silence becomes increasingly difficult to achieve. Just as moments of silence are recommended in the Liturgy, so too in the recitation of the Rosary it is fitting to pause briefly after listening to the word of God, while the mind focuses on the content of a particular mystery.

The "Our Father"

32. After listening to the word and focusing on the mystery, it is natural for the mind to be lifted up towards the Father. In each of his mysteries, Jesus always leads us to the Father, for as he rests in the Father's bosom (cf. Jn 1:18) he is continually turned towards him. He wants us to share in his intimacy with the Father, so that we can say with him: "Abba, Father" (Rom 8:15; Gal 4:6). By virtue of his relationship to the Father he makes us brothers and sisters of himself and of one another, communicating to us the Spirit which is both his and the Father's. Acting as a kind of foundation for the Christological and Marian meditation which unfolds in the repetition of the Hail Mary, the Our Father makes meditation upon the mystery, even when carried out in solitude, an ecclesial experience.

The ten "Hail Marys"

33. This is the most substantial element in the Rosary and also the one which makes it a Marian prayer par excellence. Yet when the Hail

Mary is properly understood, we come to see clearly that its Marian character is not opposed to its Christological character, but that it actually emphasizes and increases it. The first part of the Hail Mary, drawn from the words spoken to Mary by the Angel Gabriel and by Saint Elizabeth, is a contemplation in adoration of the mystery accomplished in the Virgin of Nazareth. These words express, so to speak, the wonder of heaven and earth; they could be said to give us a glimpse of God's own wonderment as he contemplates his "masterpiece"—the Incarnation of the Son in the womb of the Virgin Mary. If we recall how, in the Book of Genesis, God "saw all that he had made" (Gn 1:31), we can find here an echo of that "pathos with which God, at the dawn of creation, looked upon the work of his hands".[36] The repetition of the Hail Mary in the Rosary gives us a share in God's own wonder and pleasure: in jubilant amazement we acknowledge the greatest miracle of history. Mary's prophecy here finds its fulfilment: "Henceforth all generations will call me blessed" (Lk 1:48). The center of gravity in the Hail Mary, the hinge as it were which joins its two parts, is the name of Jesus. Sometimes, in hurried recitation, this center of gravity can be overlooked, and with it the connection to the mystery of Christ being contemplated. Yet it is precisely the emphasis given to the name of Jesus and to his mystery that is the sign of a meaningful and fruitful recitation of the Rosary. Pope Paul VI drew attention, in his Apostolic Exhortation *Marialis Cultus,* to the custom in certain regions of highlighting the name of Christ by the addition of a clause referring to the mystery being contemplated.[37] This is a praiseworthy custom, especially during public recitation. It gives forceful expression to our faith in Christ, directed to the different moments of the Redeemer's life. It is at once a profession of faith and an aid in concentrating our meditation, since it facilitates the process of assimilation to the mystery of Christ inherent in the repetition of the Hail

Mary. When we repeat the name of Jesus—the only name given to us by which we may hope for salvation (cf. Acts 4:12)—in close association with the name of his Blessed Mother, almost as if it were done at her suggestion, we set out on a path of assimilation meant to help us enter more deeply into the life of Christ. From Mary's uniquely privileged relationship with Christ, which makes her the Mother of God, *Theotókos,* derives the forcefulness of the appeal we make to her in the second half of the prayer, as we entrust to her maternal intercession our lives and the hour of our death.

The "Gloria"

34. Trinitarian doxology is the goal of all Christian contemplation. For Christ is the way that leads us to the Father in the Spirit. If we travel this way to the end, we repeatedly encounter the mystery of the three divine Persons, to whom all praise, worship and thanksgiving are due. It is important that the Gloria, the high-point of contemplation, be given due prominence in the Rosary. In public recitation it could be sung, as a way of giving proper emphasis to the essentially Trinitarian structure of all Christian prayer. To the extent that meditation on the mystery is attentive and profound, and to the extent that it is enlivened—from one Hail Mary to another—by love for Christ and for Mary, the glorification of the Trinity at the end of each decade, far from being a perfunctory conclusion, takes on its proper contemplative tone, raising the mind as it were to the heights of heaven and enabling us in some way to relive the experience of Tabor, a foretaste of the contemplation yet to come: "It is good for us to be here!" (Lk 9:33).

The concluding short prayer

35. In current practice, the Trinitarian doxology is followed by a brief concluding prayer which varies according to local custom. Without in

any way diminishing the value of such invocations, it is worthwhile to note that the contemplation of the mysteries could better express their full spiritual fruitfulness if an effort were made to conclude each mystery with a prayer for the fruits specific to that particular mystery. In this way the Rosary would better express its connection with the Christian life. One fine liturgical prayer suggests as much, inviting us to pray that, by meditation on the mysteries of the Rosary, we may come to "imitate what they contain and obtain what they promise".[38] Such a final prayer could take on a legitimate variety of forms, as indeed it already does. In this way the Rosary can be better adapted to different spiritual traditions and different Christian communities. It is to be hoped, then, that appropriate formulas will be widely circulated, after due pastoral discernment and possibly after experimental use in centers and shrines particularly devoted to the Rosary, so that the People of God may benefit from an abundance of authentic spiritual riches and find nourishment for their personal contemplation.

The Rosary beads
36. The traditional aid used for the recitation of the Rosary is the set of beads. At the most superficial level, the beads often become a simple counting mechanism to mark the succession of Hail Marys. Yet they can also take on a symbolism which can give added depth to contemplation. Here the first thing to note is the way the beads converge upon the Crucifix, which both opens and closes the unfolding sequence of prayer. The life and prayer of believers is centred upon Christ. Everything begins from him, everything leads towards him, everything, through him, in the Holy Spirit, attains to the Father. As a counting mechanism, marking the progress of the prayer, the beads evoke the unending path of contemplation and of Christian perfection. Blessed Bartolo Longo saw them also as a "chain" which links us

to God. A chain, yes, but a sweet chain; for sweet indeed is the bond to God who is also our Father. A "filial" chain which puts us in tune with Mary, the "handmaid of the Lord" (Lk 1:38) and, most of all, with Christ himself, who, though he was in the form of God, made himself a "servant" out of love for us (Phil 2:7). A fine way to expand the symbolism of the beads is to let them remind us of our many relationships, of the bond of communion and fraternity which unites us all in Christ.

The opening and closing

37. At present, in different parts of the Church, there are many ways to introduce the Rosary. In some places, it is customary to begin with the opening words of Psalm 70: "O God, come to my aid; O Lord, make haste to help me", as if to nourish in those who are praying a humble awareness of their own insufficiency. In other places, the Rosary begins with the recitation of the Creed, as if to make the profession of faith the basis of the contemplative journey about to be undertaken. These and similar customs, to the extent that they prepare the mind for contemplation, are all equally legitimate. The Rosary is then ended with a prayer for the intentions of the Pope, as if to expand the vision of the one praying to embrace all the needs of the Church. It is precisely in order to encourage this ecclesial dimension of the Rosary that the Church has seen fit to grant indulgences to those who recite it with the required dispositions. If prayed in this way, the Rosary truly becomes a spiritual itinerary in which Mary acts as Mother, Teacher and Guide, sustaining the faithful by her powerful intercession. Is it any wonder, then, that the soul feels the need, after saying this prayer and experiencing so profoundly the motherhood of Mary, to burst forth in praise of the Blessed Virgin, either in that splendid prayer the *Salve Regina* or in the *Litany of Loreto?* This is the crowning

moment of an inner journey which has brought the faithful into living contact with the mystery of Christ and his Blessed Mother.

Distribution over time

38. The Rosary can be recited in full every day, and there are those who most laudably do so. In this way it fills with prayer the days of many a contemplative, or keeps company with the sick and the elderly who have abundant time at their disposal. Yet it is clear—and this applies all the more if the new series of *mysteria lucis* is included—that many people will not be able to recite more than a part of the Rosary, according to a certain weekly pattern. This weekly distribution has the effect of giving the different days of the week a certain spiritual "color", by analogy with the way in which the Liturgy colors the different seasons of the liturgical year. According to current practice, Monday and Thursday are dedicated to the "joyful mysteries", Tuesday and Friday to the "sorrowful mysteries", and Wednesday, Saturday and Sunday to the "glorious mysteries". Where might the "mysteries of light" be inserted? If we consider that the "glorious mysteries" are said on both Saturday and Sunday, and that Saturday has always had a special Marian flavour, the second weekly meditation on the "joyful mysteries", mysteries in which Mary's presence is especially pronounced, could be moved to Saturday. Thursday would then be free for meditating on the "mysteries of light". This indication is not intended to limit a rightful freedom in personal and community prayer, where account needs to be taken of spiritual and pastoral needs and of the occurrence of particular liturgical celebrations which might call for suitable adaptations. What is really important is that the Rosary should always be seen and experienced as a path of contemplation. In the Rosary, in a way similar to what takes place in the Liturgy, the Christian week, centered on Sunday, the day of Resurrection, becomes

a journey through the mysteries of the life of Christ, and he is revealed in the lives of his disciples as the Lord of time and of history.

CONCLUSION

"Blessed Rosary of Mary, sweet chain linking us to God"

39. What has been said so far makes abundantly clear the richness of this traditional prayer, which has the simplicity of a popular devotion but also the theological depth of a prayer suited to those who feel the need for deeper contemplation. The Church has always attributed particular efficacy to this prayer, entrusting to the Rosary, to its choral recitation and to its constant practice, the most difficult problems. At times when Christianity itself seemed under threat, its deliverance was attributed to the power of this prayer, and Our Lady of the Rosary was acclaimed as the one whose intercession brought salvation. Today I willingly entrust to the power of this prayer—as I mentioned at the beginning—the cause of peace in the world and the cause of the family.

Peace

40. The grave challenges confronting the world at the start of this new Millennium lead us to think that only an intervention from on high, capable of guiding the hearts of those living in situations of conflict and those governing the destinies of nations, can give reason to hope for a brighter future. The Rosary is by its nature a prayer for peace, since it consists in the contemplation of Christ, the Prince of Peace, the one who is "our peace" (Eph 2:14). Anyone who assimilates the mystery of Christ—and this is clearly the goal of the Rosary—learns the secret of peace and makes it his life's project. Moreover, by virtue of its meditative character, with the tranquil succession of Hail Marys, the Rosary has a peaceful effect on those who pray it, disposing them to

receive and experience in their innermost depths, and to spread around them, that true peace which is the special gift of the Risen Lord (cf. Jn 14:27; 20:21). The Rosary is also a prayer for peace because of the fruits of charity which it produces. When prayed well in a truly meditative way, the Rosary leads to an encounter with Christ in his mysteries and so cannot fail to draw attention to the face of Christ in others, especially in the most afflicted. How could one possibly contemplate the mystery of the Child of Bethlehem, in the joyful mysteries, without experiencing the desire to welcome, defend and promote life, and to shoulder the burdens of suffering children all over the world? How could one possibly follow in the footsteps of Christ the Revealer, in the mysteries of light, without resolving to bear witness to his "Beatitudes" in daily life? And how could one contemplate Christ carrying the Cross and Christ Crucified, without feeling the need to act as a "Simon of Cyrene" for our brothers and sisters weighed down by grief or crushed by despair? Finally, how could one possibly gaze upon the glory of the Risen Christ or of Mary Queen of Heaven, without yearning to make this world more beautiful, more just, more closely conformed to God's plan? In a word, by focusing our eyes on Christ, the Rosary also makes us peacemakers in the world. By its nature as an insistent choral petition in harmony with Christ's invitation to "pray ceaselessly" (Lk 18:1), the Rosary allows us to hope that, even today, the difficult "battle" for peace can be won. Far from offering an escape from the problems of the world, the Rosary obliges us to see them with responsible and generous eyes, and obtains for us the strength to face them with the certainty of God's help and the firm intention of bearing witness in every situation to "love, which binds everything together in perfect harmony" (Col 3:14).

The family: parents ...

41. As a prayer for peace, the Rosary is also, and always has been, a prayer of and for the family. At one time this prayer was particularly dear to Christian families, and it certainly brought them closer together. It is important not to lose this precious inheritance. We need to return to the practice of family prayer and prayer for families, continuing to use the Rosary. In my Apostolic Letter *Novo Millennio Ineunte* I encouraged the celebration of the *Liturgy of the Hours* by the lay faithful in the ordinary life of parish communities and Christian groups;[39] I now wish to do the same for the Rosary. These two paths of Christian contemplation are not mutually exclusive; they complement one another. I would therefore ask those who devote themselves to the pastoral care of families to recommend heartily the recitation of the Rosary. The family that prays together stays together. The Holy Rosary, by age-old tradition, has shown itself particularly effective as a prayer which brings the family together. Individual family members, in turning their eyes towards Jesus, also regain the ability to look one another in the eye, to communicate, to show solidarity, to forgive one another and to see their covenant of love renewed in the Spirit of God. Many of the problems facing contemporary families, especially in economically developed societies, result from their increasing difficulty in communicating. Families seldom manage to come together, and the rare occasions when they do are often taken up with watching television. To return to the recitation of the family Rosary means filling daily life with very different images, images of the mystery of salvation: the image of the Redeemer, the image of his most Blessed Mother. The family that recites the Rosary together reproduces something of the atmosphere of the household of Nazareth: its members place Jesus at the center, they share his joys and sorrows, they place their needs and their plans in his hands, they draw from him the hope and the strength to go on.

... and children.

42. It is also beautiful and fruitful to entrust to this prayer the growth and development of children. Does the Rosary not follow the life of Christ, from his conception to his death, and then to his Resurrection and his glory? Parents are finding it ever more difficult to follow the lives of their children as they grow to maturity. In a society of advanced technology, of mass communications and globalization, everything has become hurried, and the cultural distance between generations is growing ever greater. The most diverse messages and the most unpredictable experiences rapidly make their way into the lives of children and adolescents, and parents can become quite anxious about the dangers their children face. At times parents suffer acute disappointment at the failure of their children to resist the seductions of the drug culture, the lure of an unbridled hedonism, the temptation to violence, and the manifold expressions of meaninglessness and despair. To pray the Rosary for children, and even more, with children, training them from their earliest years to experience this daily "pause for prayer" with the family, is admittedly not the solution to every problem, but it is a spiritual aid which should not be underestimated. It could be objected that the Rosary seems hardly suited to the taste of children and young people of today. But perhaps the objection is directed to an impoverished method of praying it. Furthermore, without prejudice to the Rosary's basic structure, there is nothing to stop children and young people from praying it—either within the family or in groups— with appropriate symbolic and practical aids to understanding and appreciation. Why not try it? With God's help, a pastoral approach to youth which is positive, impassioned and creative—as shown by the World Youth Days!—is capable of achieving quite remarkable results. If the Rosary is well presented, I am sure that young people will once more surprise adults by the way they make this prayer their

own and recite it with the enthusiasm typical of their age group.

The Rosary, a treasure to be rediscovered

43. Dear brothers and sisters! A prayer so easy and yet so rich truly deserves to be rediscovered by the Christian community. Let us do so, especially this year, as a means of confirming the direction outlined in my Apostolic Letter *Novo Millennio Ineunte,* from which the pastoral plans of so many particular Churches have drawn inspiration as they look to the immediate future. I turn particularly to you, my dear brother bishops, priests and deacons, and to you, pastoral agents in your different ministries: through your own personal experience of the beauty of the Rosary, may you come to promote it with conviction. I also place my trust in you, theologians: by your sage and rigorous reflection, rooted in the word of God and sensitive to the lived experience of the Christian people, may you help them to discover the Biblical foundations, the spiritual riches and the pastoral value of this traditional prayer. I count on you, consecrated men and women, called in a particular way to contemplate the face of Christ at the school of Mary. I look to all of you, brothers and sisters of every state of life, to you, Christian families, to you, the sick and elderly, and to you, young people: confidently take up the Rosary once again. Rediscover the Rosary in the light of Scripture, in harmony with the Liturgy, and in the context of your daily lives. May this appeal of mine not go unheard! At the start of the twenty-fifth year of my Pontificate, I entrust this Apostolic Letter to the loving hands of the Virgin Mary, prostrating myself in spirit before her image in the splendid Shrine built for her by Blessed Bartolo Longo, the apostle of the Rosary. I willingly make my own the touching words with which he concluded his well-known *Supplication to the Queen of the Holy Rosary:* "O Blessed Rosary of Mary, sweet chain which unites us to God, bond of love

which unites us to the angels, tower of salvation against the assaults of Hell, safe port in our universal shipwreck, we will never abandon you. You will be our comfort in the hour of death: yours our final kiss as life ebbs away. And the last word from our lips will be your sweet name, O Queen of the Rosary of Pompei, O dearest Mother, O Refuge of Sinners, O Sovereign Consoler of the Afflicted. May you be everywhere blessed, today and always, on earth and in heaven". From the Vatican, on the 16th day of October in the year 2002, the beginning of the twenty-fifth year of my Pontificate.

JOHN PAUL II

(1) Pastoral Constitution on the Church in the Modern World *Gaudium et Spes,* 45.
(2) Pope Paul VI, Apostolic Exhortation *Marialis Cultus* (2 February 1974), 42: AAS 66 (1974), 153.
(3) Cf. *Acta Leonis XIII,* 3 (1884), 280-289.
(4) Particularly worthy of note is his Apostolic Epistle on the Rosary *Il religioso convegno* (29 September 1961): AAS 53 (1961), 641-647.
(5) Angelus: *Insegnamenti di Giovanni Paolo II,* I (1978): 75-76.
(6) AAS 93 (2001), 285.
(7) During the years of preparation for the Council, Pope John XXIII did not fail to encourage the Christian community to recite the Rosary for the success of this ecclesial event: cf. Letter to the Cardinal Vicar (28 September 1960): AAS 52 (1960), 814-816.
(8) Dogmatic Constitution on the Church *Lumen Gentium,* 66.
(9) No. 32: AAS 93 (2001), 288.
(10) Ibid., 33: loc. cit., 289.
(11) It is well-known and bears repeating that private revelations are

not the same as public revelation, which is binding on the whole Church. It is the task of the Magisterium to discern and recognize the authenticity and value of private revelations for the piety of the faithful.

(12)   *The Secret of the Rosary.*

(13)   Blessed Bartolo Longo, *Storia del Santuario di Pompei,* Pompei, 1990, 59.

(14)   Apostolic Exhortation *Marialis Cultus* (2 February 1974), 47: AAS (1974), 156.

(15)   Constitution on the Sacred Liturgy *Sacrosanctum Concilium,* 10.

(16)   Ibid., 12.

(17)   Second Vatican Ecumenical Council, Dogmatic Constitution on the Church *Lumen Gentium,* 58.

(18)   *I Quindici Sabati del Santissimo Rosario,* 27th ed., Pompei, 1916, 27.

(19)   Second Vatican Ecumenical Council, Dogmatic Constitution on the Church *Lumen Gentium,* 53.

(20)   Ibid., 60.

(21)   Cf. First Radio Address *Urbi et Orbi* (17 October 1978): AAS 70 (1978), 927.

(22)   *Treatise on True Devotion to the Blessed Virgin Mary.*

(23)   *Catechism of the Catholic Church,* 2679.

(24)   Ibid., 2675.

(25)   *The Supplication to the Queen of the Holy Rosary* was composed by Blessed Bartolo Longo in 1883 in response to the appeal of Pope Leo XIII, made in his first Encyclical on the Rosary, for the spiritual commitment of all Catholics in combating social ills. It is solemnly recited twice yearly, in May and October.

(26)   *Divina Commedia,* Paradiso XXXIII, 13-15.

(27) John Paul II, Apostolic Letter *Novo Millennio Ineunte* (6 January
      2001), 20: AAS 93 (2001), 279.

(28) Apostolic Exhortation *Marialis Cultus* (2 February 1974), 46:
      AAS 6 (1974), 155.

(29) John Paul II, Apostolic Letter *Novo Millennio Ineunte* (6 January
      2001), 28: AAS 93 (2001), 284.

(30) No. 515.

(31) Angelus Message of 29 October 1978 : *Insegnamenti,* I (1978),
      76.

(32) Second Vatican Ecumenical Council, Pastoral Constitution on
      the Church in the Modern World *Gaudium et Spes,* 22.

(33) Cf. Saint Irenaeus of Lyons, *Adversus Haereses,* III, 18, 1: PG 7,
      932.

(34) *Catechism of the Catholic Church,* 2616.

(35) Cf. No. 33: AAS 93 (2001), 289.

(36) John Paul II, *Letter to Artists* (4 April 1999), 1: AAS 91 (1999),
      1155.

(37) Cf. No. 46: AAS 66 (1974), 155. This custom has also been
      recently praised by the Congregation for Divine Worship and
      for the Discipline of the Sacraments in its *Direttorio su pietà
      popolare e liturgia. Principi e orientamenti* (17 December 2001),
      201, Vatican City, 2002, 165.

(38) "...concede, quaesumus, ut haec mysteria sacratissimo beatae
      Mariae Virginis Rosario recolentes, et imitemur quod conti-
      nent, et quod promittunt assequamur." Missale Romanum,
      1960, in festo B.M. Virginis a Rosario.

(39) Cf. No. 34: AAS 93 (2001), 290.

Notes

Introduction: The New Mysteries

1. John Paul II, *Rosarium Virginis Mariae* (hereafter cited as *RVM*), 4.
2. Cited in C. Grossman, "Pope Revamps Rosary for a New Generation" in *USA Today* (October 17, 2002), section D, 11.
3. *RVM,* 19.
4. *RVM,* 40. Emphasis added.
5. *RVM,* 40.
6. *RVM,* 6.
7. *RVM,* 41.
8. *RVM,* 41.
9. *RVM,* 41.
10. *RVM,* 41.
11. *RVM,* 42.
12. *RVM,* 25.
13. *RVM,* 2.

Chapter One
Common Questions About Mary and the Rosary

1. The reason any of our prayers are efficacious is that we pray in the name of Jesus Christ. All prayerful intercession takes place through the mediation of the one mediator, Christ. Thus, the fact that we can pray for each other as Christians actually

manifests even more brilliantly the power of Christ's mediation. The same is true with Mary's intercession for us. As the *Catechism of the Catholic Church (CCC)* explains: "Mary's function ... in no way obscures or diminishes this unique mediation of Christ, but rather shows its power. But the Blessed Virgin's salutary influence on men ... flows forth from the superabundance of the merits of Christ, rests on his mediation, depends entirely on it, and draws all its power from it" (*CCC*, 970).

2. In fact, the *Catechism of the Catholic Church* teaches that living in communion with the saints leads us closer to Jesus. "Exactly as Christian communion among our fellow pilgrims brings us closer to Christ, so our communion with the saints joins us to Christ, from whom as from its fountain and head issues all grace, and the life of the People of God itself" (*CCC*, 957).

3. *RVM,* 26.

4. *RVM,* 33.

5. *RVM,* 33.

6. Robert Barron, *The Strangest Way: Walking the Christian Path* (New York: Orbis, 2002), 56.

7. *RVM,* 26.

8. Paul VI, *Marialis Cultus (MC),* 47.

9. Barron, 55.

10. *RVM,* 1.

11. *RVM,* 13.

12. *MC,* 46; *RVM,* 18.

13. *RVM,* 19.

14. *RVM,* 19.

15. *RVM,* 19.

Chapter Two
Discovering the Rosary's Soul:
Ten Practical Insights for Greater Devotion

1. *RVM*, 29.
2. *RVM*, 29.
3. *RVM*, 30.
4. *RVM*, 30.
5. See *RVM*, 32.
6. *RVM*, 32.
7. *RVM*, 33.
8. *RVM*, 33.
9. *RVM*, 10.
10. *RVM*, 14.
11. *RVM*, 14.
12. *RVM*, 34.
13. *RVM*, 35.
14. *RVM*, 36.
15. *RVM*, 36.
16. *RVM*, 37.
17. *RVM*, 25, 38.

Chapter Three
Scriptural Reflections on the Joyful Mysteries

1. *RVM,* 20.
2. John Paul II, General Audience of May 8, 1996, in John Paul II, *Theotókos: Woman, Mother, Disciple* (Boston: Pauline, 2000), 88. Also, John Paul II, *Redemptoris Mater (RM),* 8.
3. *RM,* 10.

4. John Paul II, General Audience of September 4, 1996, in *Theotókos*, 134–35.

5. *RM*, 36.

6. John Paul II, General Audience of November 20, 1996, in *Theotókos*, 145–47.

7. See S. Hahn & C. Mitch, *Ignatius Catholic Study Bible: The Gospel of Luke* (San Francisco: Ignatius, 2001), at Lk 2:7.

8. *RM*, 16.

9. *RM*, 18.

10. R. Guardini, *The Rosary of Our Lady* (Manchester, N.H.: Sophia Institute Press, 1994), 94–95.

Chapter Four

Scriptural Reflections on the Luminous Mysteries

1. St. Thomas Aquinas, *Commentary on the Gospel of St. John* (Albany, N.Y.: Magi, 1980), 152.

2. *RM*, 21.

3. St. Irenaeus, *Against the Heresies* II, 22, 4, J. Saward, trans., quoted in H. Von Balthasar, ed., *The Scandal of the Incarnation* (San Francisco: Ignatius, 1990), 61.

4. John Paul II, General Audience of February 26, 1997, in *Theotókos*, 175.

5. Bernard of Clairvaux, *On the Song of Songs*, Sermon 36:6, in K. Walsh, trans., *On the Song of Songs II*, (Kalamazoo, Mich.: Cistercian, 1976), 179.

6. *RVM*, 21.

7. Byzantine Liturgy, Feast of the Transfiguration, *Kontakion*. As cited in *CCC*, 555.

Chapter Five
Scriptural Reflections on the Sorrowful Mysteries

1. *RVM,* 22.
2. *RVM,* 22.
3. *RVM,* 22.
4. R. Brown, *Death of the Messiah* (New York: Doubleday, 1994), 189.
5. Brown, *Death of the Messiah,* 866.
6. N. Wright, *Jesus and the Victory of God* (Minneapolis: Fortress, 1996), 568.
7. Cicero, "In Defense of Rabirius," 16 in *The Speeches of Cicero,* trans. H. Hodge (Cambridge, Mass: Harvard, 1952), 467.
8. *RM,* 23.

Chapter Six
Scriptural Reflections on the Glorious Mysteries

1. *RVM,* 23.
2. Barron, 96.
3. Philo, *On the Decalogue,* 46 in C. Yonge, trans., *The Works of Philo* (Peabody, Mass: Hendrickson, 1993), 522. See also L. Johnson, *The Acts of the Apostles* (Collegeville, Minn.: Liturgical Press, 1992), 46.
4. See R. Brown, *An Introduction to the New Testament* (New York: Doubleday, 1997), 283–84; L. Johnson, 45–46; S. Pimentel, *Witnesses of the Messiah* (Steubenville, Ohio: Emmaus Road, 2002), 29–30.

5. Vatican Council II, Dogmatic Constitution on the Church (*Lumen Gentium*), 59.

6. John Paul II, General Audience of May 28, 1997, in *Theotókos*, 198–99.

7. Ignace De La Potterie, *Mary in the Mystery of the Covenant* (New York: Alba House, 1992), 17–20. While this passage might point in the direction of the Immaculate Conception, it does not by itself prove it, for Gabriel does not say, "Hail, you who have been graced since the moment of your conception." He simply says, "Hail, graced one," or even more literally, "Hail, you who have been and are now graced."

8. John Paul II, General Audience of June 25, 1997, in *Theotókos*, 201.

9. Pius XII, *Munificentissimus Deus*, as translated in *Our Lady*, ed. Benedictine Monks of Solesmes (Boston: St. Paul Editions, 1961).

10. Pius XII, 26.

11. Francis de Sales, "Sermon for the Feast of the Assumption," as cited in Pius XII, 35.

12. Pius XII, 27.

13. "The fact that Solomon denies the request in no way discredits the influence of the Gebirah [the queen mother]. Adonijah wanted Abishag the Shunammite for the treacherous purpose of taking over the kingdom from Solomon. (Taking the king's concubine was a sign of usurping the throne in the ancient Near East. For example see how Absalom, in his attempt to take the throne from David, took his concubines [2 Sm 16:20-23].) Thus the wickedness of Adonijah's intention is the reason for denial, which in no way reflects negatively upon the Gebirah's power to intercede. The narrative bears out the fact that the king normally accepted the Gebirah's request. Thus Solomon says, 'Ask, I will not refuse you.' To say then that this illustrates

the weakness of the Gebirah's ability to intercede would be to miss the whole point of the narrative, which tells how Adonijah uses the queen mother's position in an attempt to become king." T. Gray, "God's Word and Mary's Royal Office," *Miles Immaculatae* 13 (1995), 381, n. 16.

14. See my note in "Treat Her Like a Queen," in L. Suprenant, ed., *Catholic for a Reason II* (Steubenville, Ohio: Emmaus Road, 2000), 94, n. 7: "Although the identification of Mary as the 'woman' of Revelation may seem self-evident, some have interpreted this woman as merely a symbol either for the Old Testament People of Israel or for the New Testament Church. They conclude that the woman is not an individual (i.e., Mary), but only a symbol for God's people. However, this 'either-or' proposition is foreign to the Biblical world-view in which individuals often symbolically represent collective groups (e.g., Adam represented all humanity—Rom 5:19; Jacob stood for all of Israel—Ps 44:4). Given this Biblical notion called 'corporate personality,' the woman in Revelation 12 should be understood as *both* an individual (Mary) *and* a symbol for the People of God. Finally, since the other two main characters in this vision are generally recognized primarily as individuals (the child = Jesus; the dragon = the devil), it seems quite unlikely that the third main character, the woman, is not an individual, but only a symbol for a corporate group. Rather, recognizing the woman as Mary makes the most sense out of the text and at the same time is open to viewing her ... as a symbol for Israel or the Church."

15. John Paul II, General Audience of July 23, 1997, in *Theotókos*, 211–12.